BEGINNER'S GUIDE TO

Aquariums

Written by
Ed Bauman

Consultant:
Paul Victor Loiselle, Ph.D.

PUBLICATIONS INTERNATIONAL, LTD.

Louis Weber, C.E.O.
Publications International, Ltd.
7373 North Cicero Avenue
Lincolnwood, Illinois 60646

ISBN 1-56173-289-3

Biographies:

Writer Ed Bauman is the editor of *Aquarium Fish* magazine and is a longtime aquarium hobbyist. He also enjoys studying evolutionary biology and ecology.

Consultant Paul Loiselle holds a Ph.D. in Zoology from the University of California, Berkeley, and is the Assistant Curator of Freshwater Fish at the New York Aquarium. He has served as a research associate at the American Museum of Natural History, New York, and has been widely published during his 25 years as an aquarist.

Special thanks to Mike and Jan Sergey for allowing us to photograph the items in their store, The Living Sea Aquarium in Park Ridge, Illinois, and for their extended cooperation throughout this project.

Picture credits:

Educational Images: 31; **Sam Griffith Photography:** 5, 8 (bottom), 9, 16, 18, 23, 24, 26, 29, 30, 31, 32 (center, bottom left & bottom right), 36, 37, 39 (bottom), 41; **International Stock Photography:** 33; **Zig Leszczynski:** Back cover, Table of contents (bottom), 27 (top), 34, 39 (center), 42, 45 (bottom), 47 (center), 48 (bottom), 50 (top), 51 (top), 52 (top & center), 53 (center); **Paul Loiselle:** Table of contents (center), 35, 44 (bottom), 48 (top), 62 (center); **Aaron Norman:** Front cover (top & bottom left), Table of contents (top), 4, 8 (top), 11, 13, 15, 19 (bottom), 25, 32 (top), 38, 44 (center), 45 (top & center), 46, 47 (top), 48 (center), 49, 50 (center & bottom), 51 (center & bottom), 52 (bottom), 53 (bottom), 54, 55, 56, 57, 58, 59, 60, 61, 62 (top & bottom), 63 (top & bottom); **John J. O'Malley:** 14, 63 (center); **Mella Panzella:** Front cover (top right), 27 (bottom), 47 (bottom), 53 (top); **Perfecto Manufacturing:** 7, 10, 12.

Illustrations:

Jack Graber/The Creative Advantage, Inc.: Front cover (center), 6, 17, 19 (top), 21, 22, 40, 43.

Other illustrations: Lorie Robare: Assistant; Gene Schaffer

TABLE OF CONTENTS

Introduction

A freshwater community aquarium

Fishkeeping is one of the most popular leisure-time activities in the world. Millions of people have discovered the enjoyment, satisfaction, and relaxation that come from maintaining aquariums stocked with colorful tropical fish.

The hobby has intrigued people for centuries. Its roots may reach back all the way to ancient Egypt. In the Orient over a thousand years ago, people selectively bred certain goldfish for their particular beauty when viewed from above. By the middle of the 1800s, Europeans were enjoying goldfish in large wrought-iron aquariums, and at the turn of the century, aquariums became quite popular in the United States. In the following decades, technology allowed the limits of the hobby to expand, and it became increasingly popular.

Today, there are many reasons for keeping aquariums. As educational tools, they provide a first-hand look at nature. We can learn much about fish and their behavior by studying them informally in an aquarium, and we can develop a new respect for their value and beauty.

This hobby also offers many levels of involvement, any of which can be satisfying and fun. You can remain a casual hobbyist or become deeply involved in all aspects of fishkeeping. The amount of time, effort, and money invested is up to you.

Watching fish is very relaxing. Studies show that the sight of fish swimming quietly in their aquatic home lowers respiration and pulse rates, reduces tension, and provides relief from the stresses of our busy lives.

No matter how small your home, you can always find room for an aquarium, and fish make ideal pets. They are quiet, they don't need to be let outside or taken for walks, they will not damage walls or furniture, and they can be left for a week or two without problem when you go on vacation.

Fishkeeping is a wonderful hobby, but it can be a trying experience for newcomers. The apparent simplicity of a glass tank, water, and some fish is deceiving. While keeping an aquarium is not difficult, it does require some small knowledge of fish and their biological needs. Without that knowledge, it is much more difficult to succeed.

This book will focus on keeping freshwater aquariums. Saltwater aquariums are considerably more complicated to maintain and require specialized equipment in many cases. You will learn, step-by-step, everything you need to know to keep a freshwater aquarium. You will find basic information that will help you avoid common problems and mistakes that plague many novices. There is no complex science or technology here, but you'll learn some very simple biological principles, and you'll become familiar with the design and function of aquarium equipment.

CHAPTER 1

Aquarium Basics

Keeping an aquarium can provide immeasurable rewards and satisfaction. It does, however, require some work as well, and before you venture in to the hobby, you'll need some fundamental information. The best way to begin is with a basic understanding of what happens in a successful aquarium. You'll also need to know how to select a good aquarium store, one that can provide you with reliable equipment, service, and advice. Finally, you'll need to take the first step in planning your aquarium: selecting a tank and a suitable location for it.

One of the first steps in starting an aquarium is finding a good store.

The natural cycle that helps keep freshwater bodies clean involves water currents, evaporation, and precipitation.

THE CLOSED AQUATIC ENVIRONMENT

It's actually amazing that fish can survive in an aquarium at all. Compared with their natural habitats—from jungle streams to vast lakes—even a relatively large aquarium is tiny. An aquarium also has several built-in limitations that work against the health of its occupants. No matter how extravagant and no matter how carefully planned, any aquarium is an *artificial* environment.

Natural aquatic ecosystems are much more complicated than the aquatic environment of an aquarium. The biological processes in a body of water have been finely tuned over millennia to become a complex, living system. This system includes weather patterns, geological and chemical processes, and countless interrelationships among plants, animals, and microorganisms. The life-forms found in these systems have adapted to very specific conditions, and their ability to survive depends on their environment.

A closed system like an aquarium is a completely different thing. By definition, a closed system means that the environment consists solely of the tank and its contents. The natural processes that, in the wild, would provide food, protection, and a clean, uncontaminated environment for the fish are not a part of the aquarium. As a fishkeeper, your primary responsibility is to see that these things are taken care of in the confines of your aquarium.

Providing nourishment and a safe and comfortable habitat are essential, of course. Maintaining the *water quality,* however, is something a bit less obvious to most new aquarists. Water quality refers to the amount of debris, pollutants, and other undesirable substances that appear in the water either naturally or through contamination, and more aquariums fail due to poor water quality than probably anything else.

Why is water quality so important? Approximately 80 to 90 percent of all fish diseases have their source in physical stress on the fish. The most common source of stress is from living in polluted water. This stress, if persistent and unrelieved, causes the immune system of a fish to become less and less able to fight infection from disease-causing organisms that are always present in the water. Some species of fish suffer from this problem more quickly than others, but all fish eventually become sick and die when kept in poor-quality water.

Beginning aquarists can have a difficult time keeping their aquariums healthy not because they lack skill or motivation but because they lack knowledge. Keeping water clean is actually not difficult at all; it requires only a little understanding, a little effort, and the right equipment.

Water quality deteriorates for several reasons. As a part of their metabolism, fish produce various waste products that accumulate in the water, and other organic matter such as uneaten food decays into substances that can contaminate the water. Over time, these pollutants build up in an aquarium to a level that is dangerous to the occupants. In their native environment, fish are protected from this problem by a natural system. The water in a river or lake is continually replenished with fresh rainwater, and different chemical and biological processes remove organic pollutants from the water. To keep a healthy aquarium, you simply need to understand this natural system and duplicate its effects for your fish.

Prior to the advent of filtration, hobbyists depended on their ability to maintain a balance in the tank. The number and size of fish, the abundance of plants, and the ability of snails and other scavengers to consume excess food and other materials in the tank were all taken into consideration. It was, however, a balancing act that only the most skilled aquarists could maintain over time. The number of fish that could be kept in these balanced or natural aquariums was rather small. And yet, when measured against the natural environment of the fish, even these aquariums were rather overcrowded.

Today, new hobbyists often believe that aquarium technology, particularly the filtration system, eliminates the work and the problems of keeping fish. Up to a point, this is true. Certainly in comparison to keeping fish in a bowl, where all of the water must be changed at least once a week, an aquarium with a filter is more convenient and easier to maintain. Still, filtration systems have limitations.

Today's aquariums come in a variety of shapes and sizes.

A pair of angelfish

No matter how sophisticated, a filter can only slow down the rate at which the water in an aquarium becomes polluted. No filter system can actually stop water quality from deteriorating. Filtration *is* important to maintaining good water quality for the fish, and filters *do* make it possible to keep more fish in an aquarium. Success with fishkeeping, however, requires more than a good filter. The true value of filtration is that it helps you maintain good water quality more consistently, but only if some simple, easy-to-follow principles of aquarium care are followed.

The real key to success is found in three basic rules, each formulated to create a stable environment for the fish. Rule one is to not overstock the tank with fish. The more fish there are in an aquarium, the faster the water quality goes down. As noted earlier, the filter only slows this process. The second rule is to not overfeed the fish. The accumulation of uneaten food in the tank will quickly contaminate the water. Rule three is to do frequent partial water changes. This removes pollutants and adds fresh, clean water to the aquarium, helping to maintain a healthy habitat.

If you understand these three rules and the reasoning behind them, you're well on your way to becoming a successful aquarist. What remains is to learn about the equipment you'll be using—what you need and why you need it—and then to learn a little about the fish that you'll be setting up house for.

A clean, neat, well-organized aquarium store will be likely to provide complete service and support to its customers.

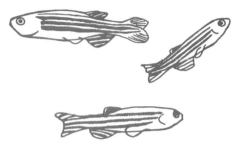

Left: *A variety of well-displayed items is one sign of a first-rate store.*

WHERE TO SHOP

New hobbyists seldom realize how valuable a good pet store is to their success in fishkeeping. Value, in this case, has nothing to do with the lowest prices or shortest driving distance. What you want is a store that can offer good advice, provide answers to problems, recommend products that will best serve your needs, and handle warranties or repairs for equipment.

If you live in an urban area, you'll probably have dozens of pet and aquarium stores to choose from. The smaller the city or the more rural your area is, the fewer shops there will be. One of your first goals is to visit as many aquarium dealers as are convenient *before* you purchase anything.

As you visit each store, there are certain things to look for. The shop should have a clean general appearance. The floors should be swept and the carpets vacuumed. Shelves should be stocked with a variety of merchandise, and everything should be clean. Dust, particularly on containers of food, means a low turnover of goods, increasing the likelihood of old or outdated products.

The tanks themselves should look well kept. The water should be clear and the front glass clean—no water spots on the outside or algae on the inside. The tanks should be clearly labeled with the names and prices of the fish contained within them.

The fish should be healthy and active; that is, individual fish should display color and behavior that is typical of the species. In a large store with many tanks, the occasional dead fish in a tank can happen. However, if many of the tanks contain dead fish, or if the employees seems uninterested when a dead fish is pointed out to them, you'll want to take your business elsewhere. If the fish aren't healthy when you buy them, they are unlikely to become healthy in your own aquarium, and they could be carrying disease that will affect your other fish

Note whether the dealer has a good selection of nice-looking live plants. Even if you end up using artificial plants, a store that stocks specialty items like good-quality live plants is much more likely to serve the needs of hobbyists at all levels. Also look for a display of aquarium books. A large and varied number of titles indicates a dealer who knows how important reading about the hobby is for aquarists—particularly beginners.

The quality of the sales staff is also important. They should be knowledgeable about the hobby in general and interested in your questions. They don't have to know the answer to every question, but they should be willing to find out what the answers are.

Do not simply patronize the shop with the lowest prices. As often as not, the shop with the lowest prices has the least knowledgeable staff, the poorest selection of merchandise, and the least healthy fish. It is always better to pay a little more to a reliable dealer who will support you and help you grow in the hobby.

Top and above: *Small tanks come in a number of different styles, and they can make a nice addition to any room. They don't hold many fish, though, and they require meticulous maintenance.*

CHOOSING AN AQUARIUM

There are three basic factors to consider before actually purchasing an aquarium. You want to decide where the tank should go, what kind of fish you want to keep in it, and how much money you feel comfortable spending. You should really make these decisions *before* bringing home a tank. Aquariums last for many years, and if you make the wrong choice, you may have to live with it for a long time.

The first thing to determine is where the tank will reside. It is important that you be able to view the aquarium easily from a favorite chair. Keeping the tank in an area where you spend a lot of your time will enhance your enjoyment of your fish and your interest in fishkeeping. Sitting comfortably and watching the fish lets you appreciate them, and it also provides an opportunity to note if they are behaving normally. Experienced aquarists can catch problems early by simply noting changes in the behavior of their fish.

The tank also has to be in a place that offers ready access. Although an aquarium doesn't require much maintenance, it does need some. If it is difficult to work around the tank because of a lack of space, you will be much more likely to put the work off and let the water quality deteriorate, and, as a result, keeping your aquarium healthy will become much more of a chore.

The location of the tank should also be determined by the room's light, temperature, and traffic. One of your goals is to provide the fish with a stable, secure environment. This is much easier to do if you can control these factors. Sunlight coming through a window or door can overheat the tank, particularly in summer, raising the water to lethal temperatures. Excess light can also cause significant algae growth in an aquarium. The combination of warm water, sunlight, and nutrients in the water encourages unwanted algae to multiply and cover every surface in the aquarium.

Nearby windows and doors can subject the tank to drafts of cold or hot air, making it harder to maintain a consistent water temperature. Rapid changes in temperature create enough stress to cause some fish to become sick. For this reason, the tank should also be kept away from radiators, vents, and other sources of hot or cold air.

Heavy traffic around the aquarium can be very disturbing to many fish. If people are continually walking by the tank or if nearby shelves or furniture receive frequent use, the unusual activity can stress the fish and make it more difficult for them to thrive.

In addition to picking the location, you must decide how you're going to display the aquarium. The tank must sit on a sturdy support. A nice table or other piece of furniture is seldom suitable except for the smallest of tanks. The weight of a typical aquarium is roughly 10 pounds per gallon, so a 10-gallon tank will weigh about 100 pounds and a 30-gallon tank will weigh about 300 pounds. Most furniture is not designed to support that kind of weight. The furniture would also suffer from the effects of spilled and splashed water, which is a virtual certainty no matter how careful you are.

For these reasons, the best way to support an aquarium is with a stand designed specifically for this purpose. These are usually made from wood or wrought iron, sometimes with a second shelf for another aquarium or for supplies and equipment. Even better are stands with doors to hide air pumps, filters, food, and other items. A good aquarium stand is a unique piece of furniture. If you are willing to spend the money, custom-crafted aquarium furniture can make the aquarium fit perfectly into the decor of any room.

The floor itself must be level and capable of withstanding the total weight of the aquarium and support. The main reason for needing a level floor is to avoid uneven stresses on the tank that might cause a leak. It also looks better if the water line is even at the top of the tank. With most tanks, weight will not be a problem. However, for very large aquariums, 100 gallons or more, some floors may have to be reinforced. One problem with most stands is that all of the weight is actually transmitted to the floor at only four points, where the legs are. It may help to distribute the weight more evenly by placing lengths of wood under the legs.

Your next concern is to choose the best size and shape of aquarium. Ideally, you want to purchase the largest tank possible—one that you can afford and that will fit into the chosen space. A larger aquarium will hold more fish, of course, but greater size will also provide a more stable aquatic environment. As the volume of water increases, it can be easier to maintain consistent water temperatures and good water quality. This is not to imply, however, that a modest-size tank will have problems. With a little care and attention, any tank of 10 gallons or more can be a healthy home for fish.

The cost of an aquarium rises moderately with its size until you pass capacities of about 55 gallons, at which point prices rise much faster. The amount of glass

A Butterfly Dwarf Cichlid

needed for very large tanks and the increased thickness required as the tanks become deeper contribute to these price increases.

The numbers and sizes of fish that can be kept are affected by both the tank size and the tank dimensions. For this reason, it may help to know what kinds of fish you want to keep when shopping for an aquarium. If you don't want to plan that far in advance, just be aware that you may have to avoid certain types of fish if your aquarium is not suitable for them. Don't worry, though; no matter what kind of tank you buy, you'll be able to choose from a great variety of potential residents.

You will discover that aquariums of similar or identical capacities can have very different dimensions. While the amount of water that an aquarium holds is important, many new hobbyists do not realize that the dimensions of a tank can be important too. The length and width of the tank determine the surface area of the water, and surface area directly affects the number and size of fish that can be kept in the aquarium.

The significance of surface area may not be clear until you understand a little more about the biology of an aquatic environment. One of the most important rules of successful fishkeeping is to not overstock your tank. Overcrowding can make it all but impossible to keep fish alive and healthy. Increasing the filter size and the amount of maintenance can partially compensate for too many fish, but in the long run nature takes it course and fish will sicken and die until the aquarium is no longer overcrowded.

Exactly what constitutes overcrowding, however, is hard to say. Looking at the tanks in stores is no help because these aquariums are vastly overstocked. The short amount of time the fish are in these tanks, combined with extensive filtration and frequent maintenance, allows retailers to maintain heavy tank populations.

For many years, aquarists have used guidelines that relate the size of the fish to the volume of the tank. The most common guide used is one inch of fish per gallon of water. This refers to adult fish and does not include the tail.

Although not a bad rule of thumb, this guideline has two major shortcomings. First of all, a fish's length does not by itself indicate the total impact the fish will have on a closed aquatic system. While some fish are slim, others have much fuller bodies. As fish grow, their weight or mass may increase much faster than their length. The end result is that an aquarium may meet the guidelines of an inch of fish for every gallon of water but still be overstocked or understocked.

The second problem with this guideline is that it doesn't account for surface area, which is a real limiting factor. Fish require oxygen to live. They remove dissolved oxygen from the water and release carbon dioxide into the water, so the dissolved oxygen content of a tank is one of the things that determines a safe stocking level. Oxygen enters the water from the atmosphere *at the surface,* and carbon dioxide is released into the atmosphere *at the surface.* The greater the surface area, the greater the exchange of oxygen and carbon dioxide and the more fish the tank can support.

Large, traditional tanks hold many fish and help to create a healthy habitat.

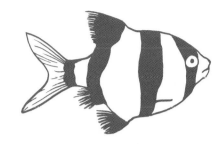

To take surface area into account, a good guideline for stocking an aquarium is one inch of adult fish (not including the tail) for every 24 square inches of surface area. This also does not account for the difference between slim and broad fish, but this rule of thumb at least provides a greater margin of safety. This guideline, by the way, is for tropical aquarium fish. Cold-water fish, such as goldfish, need 30 square inches of surface area per inch, which takes into account their much greater body mass per inch and greater oxygen requirements.

What all of this means is that when choosing an aquarium, it is best to try to select the one that has the greatest surface area for a given volume. If you choose a tank shape that offers less surface area, take that into consideration when stocking it.

Aquariums of the same capacity but different surface areas come in three basic types: regular, show, and long tanks. Show tanks tend to be taller than regular tanks, thus providing a larger front glass area to view the fish but a smaller surface area. They are narrower front to back than normal tanks. Long tanks have a greater length than regular tanks, making for a very attractive display tank and increasing the surface area. Show tanks are particularly well-suited for deep-bodied fish, such as angelfish, whereas long tanks are good choices for territorial species or for fast-swimming, schooling fish.

A different tank shape is the hexagon aquarium, with six sides. These can make very attractive displays, but keep in mind that the surface area of this type of tank is less than that for a normal tank of the same volume. Round or bubble tanks are even worse in this respect because the maximum amount of surface area is available only when the tank is half full. As the water level goes higher than this, the surface area decreases. This is the same problem that plagues goldfish bowls. Worst of all are very tall, thin aquariums, which have the surface area of a much smaller aquarium.

Top: *A Platy* Above: *A Paradise Fish*

Recently mini aquariums ranging from two to six gallons have become very popular. While they are attractive and inexpensive, these tanks can be very difficult to maintain. They hold limited amounts of water, they have only a minimal surface area, and they often come with inefficient filter systems. Even experienced fishkeepers have a very difficult time maintaining healthy fish in tanks of this size.

CHAPTER 2

Aquarium Equipment

Fishkeeping is really more of an art than a science. As a true aquarist, you'll develop an appreciation for the beauty of the hobby and a certain respect for the creatures in your tank. You'll come to view your aquarium not as a pastime or as an attractive addition to your living room, but as a delicate, vibrant system that takes shape and comes to life through your efforts, skill, and vision.

Like all arts, though, fishkeeping does have its technical side. To succeed, you have to create a suitable habitat for your fish, and to do that, you must use the proper tools. Knowing how your equipment works and why you need it will greatly increase your chances of success.

An adult male Platy

When planning your aquarium, keep in mind that you probably won't need all of the items that appear in the following pages. Consult with your dealer to determine which pieces of equipment you'll need to create the kind of aquarium you want.

FILTRATION

As soon as fish are added to an aquarium, the normal processes of respiration and digestion produce waste products that pollute the water. There are also other sources of pollution, such as decaying uneaten food. The biggest challenge in keeping an aquarium is controlling the level of these pollutants so that your fish have a healthy environment, and one of the things you need to meet that challenge is an effective filtration system.

In many ways, filtration is the most complicated and difficult aspect of fishkeeping. A visit to any well-stocked aquarium or pet store will reveal an astonishing array of filters that vary widely in design and price. In addition, the beginning aquarist faces a lot of new terms that are used to describe filters. Understanding how filters work and what they accomplish can make it much easier to sort through everything.

You may assume that the basic goal of filtration is to remove debris floating in the water so that it doesn't cause pollution. While this is correct, it's only part of the story. This process is *mechanical* filtration. If mechanical filtration is sufficient, very little solid matter will be left floating in the water. However, just because the water looks clean doesn't mean it is safe for fish. Most of the pollution that causes the water quality to deteriorate can't be seen. In order to remove it, two other types of filtration are needed: *chemical* filtration and *biological* filtration.

Only when mechanical, chemical, and biological filtration are available can a truly healthy environment be maintained for the fish. Aquarists often use two different filters together in order to provide these three types of filtration. This is because filter designs that are very good at providing one or possibly two types of filtration tend to be less effective at providing the remaining types.

A shoal of Neon Tetras

MECHANICAL FILTRATION

Mechanical filtration is accomplished by moving water through some kind of material that acts like a sieve, catching the solids and removing them from the water. Ideally, the most effective mechanical filter removes particles down to very small sizes, but there is a trade-off here. The smaller the particles are that the filter removes, the faster the filter material will clog. Because clogged filter material severely reduces the rate of water flow through it, the material must be cleaned or changed. The more effective the filter material is at trapping small particles, the more often you will have to clean the filter.

For this reason, most filter material is designed to catch only the larger, more visible solids. Of course, as the filter material catches large particles, the openings in the material through which the water flows will become increasingly smaller and thus trap increasingly smaller particles. The material does clog eventually, but it takes much longer.

CHEMICAL FILTRATION

Chemical filtration is needed because a number of dissolved, invisible compounds accumulate in aquarium water, and they can't be removed by mechanical filtra-

Granular activated carbon used for chemical filtration

tion. These compounds are not toxic to the fish but can inhibit their growth and cause chronic, low-level stress that eventually leads to disease. Most of these compounds are dissolved organic substances produced by natural biological decay.

The dissolved organic substances eventually reach concentrations high enough to become visible as a yellowish tinge in the water. You can see this when a sheet of white paper is held behind the tank so that half of it is viewed through the water. If the water is healthy for the fish, the paper viewed through the water will be as white as the other half; if not, the paper will have a yellowish cast to it.

Chemical filtration removes many, but not all, of these compounds. However, some substances that affect the growth of the fish can only be removed by making partial water changes on a regular basis. If this isn't done, the fish will never grow to normal adult size. This stunted growth will result in fish that never achieve the beauty of mature fish, and it can cause other related health problems.

There are many ways to accomplish chemical filtration, but for all practical purposes, the only method that is both effective and relatively economical is to pass the aquarium water over granular activated carbon. Granular activated carbon is usually made from an organic material, such as coconut shells, that is ground into small pieces and then heated to 2000 degrees Fahrenheit to drive off gases in the material. This "activation" produces carbon that can *adsorb* the molecules of compounds in the water and hold on to them. Adsorption is the adhesion of a thin layer of molecules to a solid (in this case, the activated carbon). The carbon eventually becomes saturated with molecules and must be replaced. It cannot be reactivated by hobbyists because of the special ovens needed for the process. Granular activated carbon should not be confused with charcoal, which is sold in some stores at a much lower price but does not provide effective chemical filtration.

There are a few things to keep in mind when using granular activated carbon. The smaller the granules of carbon, the greater the total surface area available to adsorb molecules for any given amount of carbon. The total surface area of the carbon determines how long you can wait before it is necessary to replace it. A good rule of thumb is to use one ounce of carbon for every four gallons of water. If the tank is not overstocked with fish, the carbon should last at least a month and probably twice that.

BIOLOGICAL FILTRATION

The third type of filtration—biological filtration—is the most important of all. The lack of effective biological filtration is probably responsible for the deaths of more fish than any other cause. The particular dissolved compounds controlled by biological filtration are very toxic to fish even at low concentrations. In newly set up tanks, the effects of these compounds can kill fish very quickly. In aquariums that have been running longer but are overstocked with fish, there can be constant low levels of these compounds in'the water. This creates chronic, long-term physical stress, resulting in continual problems with diseased and dying fish.

To understand biological filtration, it is necessary to understand a basic process in the aquarium: the nitrogen cycle. Ammonia is one of the key elements in the nitrogen cycle. Fish produce ammonia directly both as a by-product of respiration and as a waste product from the digestion of foods. Solid wastes are also converted into ammonia, which is why it is important to remove them with mechanical filtration. Uneaten food, plant materials, and other organic items in the tank that decay are also converted to ammonia.

Ammonia, a nitrogen-based compound, is extremely toxic. In an aquarium, it can build up quickly and threaten all the fish in the tank. Nature, as usual, has a solution to the problem. A species of bacteria known as *Nitrosomonas* will actually consume ammonia, as long as there is enough dissolved oxygen in the water to support the bacteria. *Nitrosomonas* bacteria are everywhere, so you don't even need to add them to the aquarium; they will grow there naturally. However, it takes them a while to multiply to a population size capable of consuming all the ammonia in the water.

As the *Nitrosomonas* consume the ammonia, they convert it to nitrite. Nitrite is also toxic to fish and in the long run tends to be a larger problem than ammonia. Another species of bacteria, *Nitrobacter*, will consume the nitrite and convert it to nitrate, a relatively harmless compound that can be used up by plants and algae.

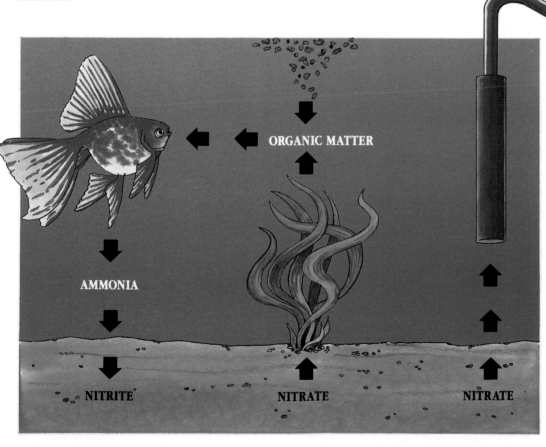

The nitrogen cycle is essential to maintaining a healthy aquarium environment.

ORGANIC MATTER

AMMONIA

NITRITE

NITRATE

NITRATE

As with *Nitrosomonas* bacteria, it takes some time before the *Nitrobacter* are able to multiply to sufficient numbers to handle all of the nitrite. Unfortunately, until the *Nitrosomonas* are able to increase to numbers sufficient to control the ammonia in a new aquarium, the high ammonia levels inhibit the growth of *Nitrobacter*, thus allowing the nitrite levels to increase quickly and remain high. While it may take a week or less for the population of ammonia-consuming *Nitrosomonas* to grow to sufficient numbers, the delay in *Nitrobacter* growth means it can be six weeks or more before nitrite is under control.

This process of starting the nitrogen cycle, which generally takes a total of six to eight weeks, is known as "breaking in the tank." If there are too many fish in the tank during this process, and not enough water changes are made, many of the fish will die. This situation is known as "new tank syndrome." It's also the reason so many new hobbyists are unable to keep their fish alive and healthy.

Some aquarists report that they successfully break in their tanks using fish, but add a one-step water conditioner that neutralizes the toxic ammonia. The neutralized ammonia can still be consumed by the *Nitrosomonas* bacteria so they can multiply, but it will pose no danger to the fish. However, the *Nitrosomonas* bacteria will still produce nitrite, and the fish will have to battle the increasing concentrations of that chemical until the *Nitrobacter* colony is established.

The end product of the nitrogen cycle—nitrate—will not harm fish unless it reaches rather high levels. Because nitrate can be used by plants as food, live plants will help control nitrate levels. Without aquatic plants, however, the nitrate will be used as food by simpler plants—algae. One way of controlling problems with excess algae is to lower the nitrate level by making partial water changes, which should be a normal part of aquarium maintenance anyway.

AERATION AND SURFACE AGITATION

Before looking at specific filter designs, you should understand your aquarium's need for surface agitation. At the surface level, water and air undergo a natural exchange of gases. Oxygen goes from the air to the water, and carbon dioxide goes from the water to the air. This is how the oxygen that fish breathe enters their habitat and how the carbon dioxide that they produce by respiration is removed from their habitat. When the surface of aquarium water is disturbed, the rate of gas exchange between the water and the air is increased; more carbon dioxide is released into the atmosphere and more dissolved oxygen is taken by the

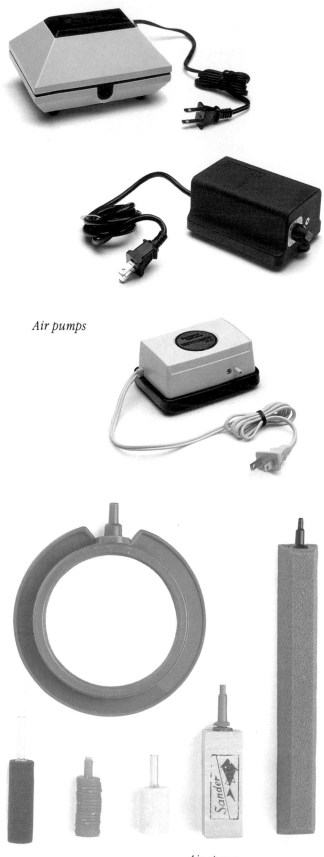

Air pumps

Air stones

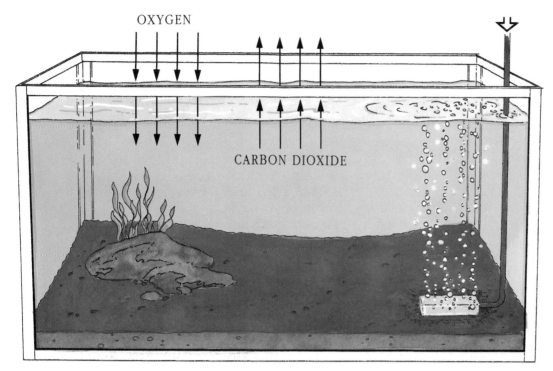

OXYGEN

CARBON DIOXIDE

Disturbing the surface water with air bubbles will allow more efficient exchange of gases; it helps to remove harmful carbon dioxide and add beneficial oxygen to the aquarium.

water. The surface tension of the water must be broken for sufficient gas exchange. Fortunately, creating surface agitation is easily done with aeration, or pumping air into the water so that it forms bubbles. The bubbles rise to the surface and burst, thus breaking the surface tension. This also creates water movement in the tank, in effect stirring the aquarium ever so slightly, so that all of the materials and compounds in the water—both the beneficial ones and the harmful ones—are evenly distributed throughout the tank.

One way of providing the necessary aeration is to use air stones connected to an air pump. The air stones can be made from wood or other highly porous materials. When air is forced in one end of the air stone by the pump, it is released as bubbles from the other end. Many filters, however, use air bubbles as a part of their design. As air bubbles move upward, their movement causes water to rise up with them, in effect creating a current that circulates all the water in the tank. These air-lift filters use this technique to pull water through their filter media and thus clean the entire tank. Any filter that uses air bubbles to operate will provide the needed aeration, as long as the bubbles are driven with enough air to actually break the surface tension of the water. Filters that do not use air bubbles to create circulation often have available attachments that provide the necessary aeration.

Pearl Gourami

FILTER DESIGNS

Mechanical filters all serve the same function, but they come in a variety of different designs: inside box filter, inside power filter, outside power filter, and canister filter. Each type of filter has its own system for creating water flow, and each type has its own advantages and disadvantages. All will work well depending on the capacity of the filter, the size of the tank, and the amount of maintenance the filter receives. Nearly all mechanical filters also have a compartment to hold activated granular carbon, so that they act as efficient chemical filters as well. To avoid having the carbon become covered with solid matter, which would keep it from adsorbing the chemical wastes, the water should pass through the mechanical filtering material *first*. That way, the solid matter will be removed from the water before it reaches the carbon.

The inside box filter is the simplest and least expensive of all mechanical filters. The filter is set up inside the aquarium itself, and it can be relatively effective in smaller tanks. Bubbles from a tube or air stone inside the box draw water through it. The bubbles rising to the surface from the box also help aerate the tank. The box itself is filled with Dacron filter material and a quantity of granular activated carbon.

There are a few drawbacks to the inside box filter. It is not very effective in large aquariums. From a visual standpoint, it adds nothing to the appearance of the tank, although it can sometimes be hidden successfully behind plants or a large rock. Also, changing the filter material requires removing the unit from the tank.

The inside power filter is similar to the box filter except that a motor pumps water through the filter at a much faster rate. The greater flow rate will act to improve filtration. As with the air-driven box filter, though, visual appearance and maintenance are drawbacks. In addition, you will probably also need air stones to provide sufficient aeration for the tank.

An outside power filter hangs on the back of the tank and has intake and outflow tubes that sit inside the tank. An outside power filter offers many advantages over internal filters. Because it is behind the tank, the filter itself cannot be seen, although the intake and outflow tubes will be somewhat visible. The boxes of these filters are large, too, so more filter material and granular activated carbon can be used, increasing the amount of mechanical and chemical filtration. Also maintenance of these filters is usually much easier because they are not submerged in the aquarium.

Some outside power filters use cartridges or bags of carbon that are prefilled by the manufacturer. If the cartridge or bag doesn't fit tightly in the space allocated for it in the filter box, the effectiveness of the chemical filtration will be reduced. This is because water takes the route of least resistance, and it will flow around the cartridge or bag if there is space rather than being forced through the carbon. To remedy this situation, slit open the cartridge or bag and fill it with more carbon. This will create a tighter fit while providing more carbon for chemical filtration.

Outside power filters also have much higher flow rates. In order for mechanical and chemical filtration to be effective, the filter should process the volume of the tank four to five times each hour. In larger tanks, these flow rates are only possible with outside power filters and canister filters.

Canister filters differ from outside power filters in that hoses transport the water from the tank through the filter and then back to the aquarium. The canister filter can sit under the tank or on a shelf, although some have optional brackets to attach the filter to the back of the tank.

As a general rule, canister filters cannot move as much water as outside power filters, primarily because of the length and diameter of the hoses. In addition, some aquarists believe that canister filters are more difficult to maintain than outside power filters.

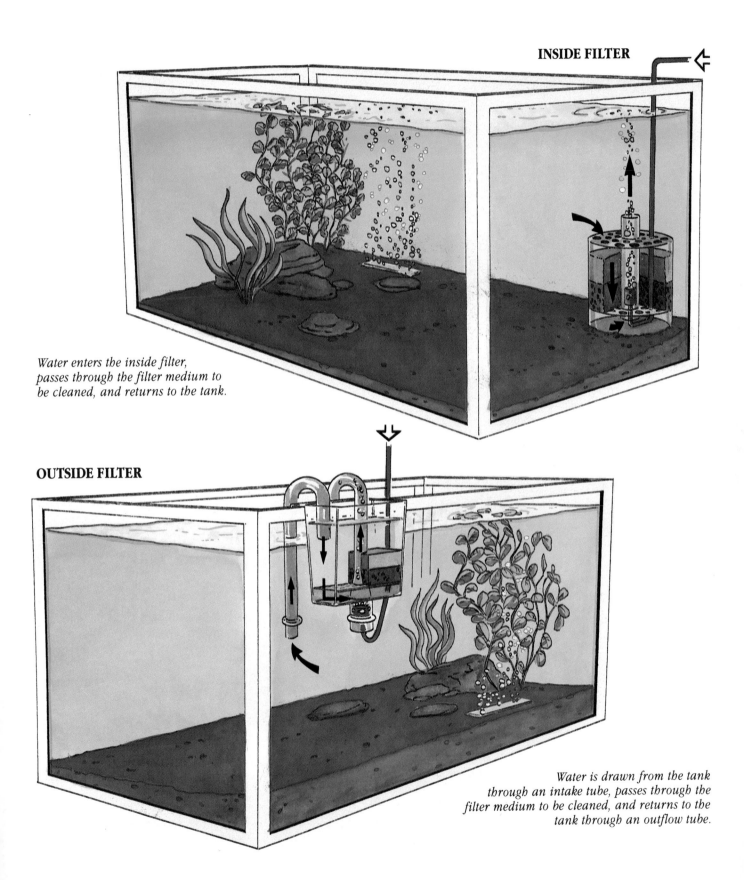

INSIDE FILTER

Water enters the inside filter, passes through the filter medium to be cleaned, and returns to the tank.

OUTSIDE FILTER

Water is drawn from the tank through an intake tube, passes through the filter medium to be cleaned, and returns to the tank through an outflow tube.

UNDERGRAVEL FILTER

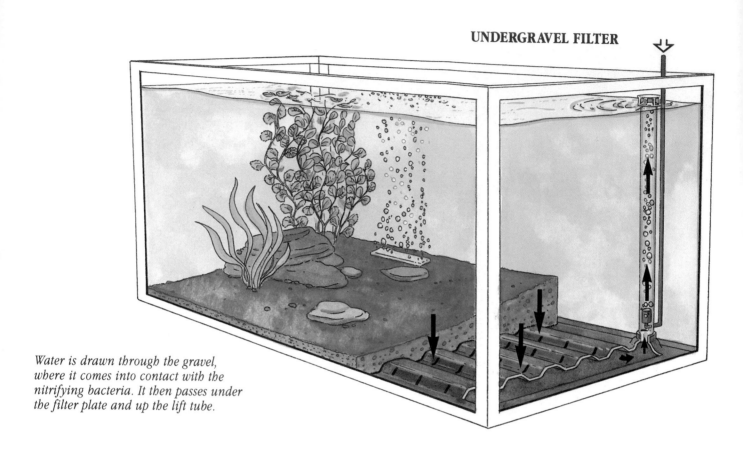

Water is drawn through the gravel, where it comes into contact with the nitrifying bacteria. It then passes under the filter plate and up the lift tube.

One unique type of canister filter is the diatomaceous earth filter. Some regular canister filters have special inserts for this purpose, whereas others are designed specifically for this kind of filtration. A very fine white powder (diatomaceous earth) is used to coat a special material in the filter through which the water flows. The filter is run for two or three hours, during which time the gravel is stirred occasionally to release any solid matter in it. Extremely small particles can be removed with this type of mechanical filtration, making the water very clear. A diatomaceous earth filter is not designed for continuous operation because the filtration material clogs within hours.

Biological filters function in a completely different way, and they have a completely different design. The *Nitrosomonas* and *Nitrobacter* bacteria necessary for biological filtration will colonize virtually every surface in a tank. However, there is usually not enough surface area in a tank to support populations of these nitrifying bacteria large enough to process all the ammonia that is produced in a typical aquarium. A biological filter deals with this problem by making the natural nitrogen cycle operate more productively.

A biological filter has two main functions. It increases the amount of surface area available to the nitrifying bacteria, and it creates a constant flow of aquarium water over the colonized area. The most popular kind of biological filter is the undergravel filter. It is relatively inexpensive, reliable, and very effective. An undergravel filter is really just a plastic plate that covers the bottom of the aquarium. The plate has many small holes or slots in it. The exact physical appearance varies from one brand to another, but all work on exactly the same principle.

The undergravel filter plate is covered with aquarium gravel. Located at each back corner of the plate is a lift tube that extends from the plate to the top of the tank. The aquarium water is drawn up the lift tube along with bubbles from an air stone at the bottom or by a small motor, called a powerhead, at the top. This pulls water from under the plate, which in turn draws water down through the gravel.

As the water passes across the grains of gravel, the nitrifying bacteria living there utilize the dissolved oxygen in the water to metabolize the ammonia and nitrite. The grains of

gravel offer a huge total surface area for the bacteria to colonize, and the steady water movement ensures that enough oxygen will be available to support the large colonies. As a result, the aquarium will house more than enough nitrifying bacteria to complete the nitrogen cycle, and the fish will have a healthy environment.

In addition to being a biological filter, the undergravel filter acts as a mechanical filter because it catches solids as they pass into the gravel bed. Unfortunately, this actually works against the biological filtration because as the spaces between the pieces of gravel fill with particles, the flow of oxygenated water past the bacteria is reduced. Over time, the effectiveness of the biological filtration is significantly impaired. This problem can be solved by using a separate mechanical filter to remove many of the particles before they become buried in the gravel bed, and by cleaning the gravel when doing water changes, which will be described in the section on aquarium maintenance.

An undergravel filter does not function as a chemical filter. Some undergravel filters are supplied with small cartridges of granular activated carbon that sit at the top of each lift tube, but these should be discarded for two reasons. First, there isn't enough carbon in these cartridges to last more than a few days at the most. Second, these cartridges reduce the flow of water through the filter significantly.

Another kind of biological filter that is commonly used in aquariums is the sponge filter. Although varying somewhat in appearance, all sponge filters work the same way. Water is pulled through the sponge, which is colonized by nitrifying bacteria. Most sponge filters use a single lift tube and air bubbles to draw water through the sponge, although some large models can utilize a powerhead instead.

There are specific reasons for using sponge filters. For example, if you keep a sponge filter in a tank that already has a biological filter, it will develop its own colony of bacteria. The sponge filter can then serve as an emergency biological filter in another tank. If you need to set up a small tank to treat a sick fish or a quarantine tank for new fish, the sponge filter can provide immediate biological filtration for that tank. This eliminates the usual break-in period.

For those who breed fish, the sponge filter is also very useful. Often at some point, young fish need to be taken out of the adult tank and put into a fry tank, which contains only juveniles of the same size. Sponge filters provide

Inside box filters

An outside power filter

Above: *A sponge filter*
Left: *A canister filter*

instant biological filtration for the fry tank. It is safe for the baby fish because there is no dangerous filter intake, as with power filters, and the micro-organisms on the surface of the sponge even provide an additional food source for the growing fish.

It should be mentioned here that all mechanical filters eventually function as biological filters. That is, the mechanical filter material and the granular activated carbon will become colonized by nitrifying bacteria. However, by the time the mechanical and chemical filtration materials are fully functioning biological filters, they will need to be removed and replaced as a normal part of filter maintenance.

The only exception to this is when foam or sponge is used as the mechanical filtering material. Then, the material can be squeezed gently several times in a bucket of aquarium water and placed back in the filter. Most of the nitrifying bacteria will survive this procedure and reform the colony.

Because outside power filters and canister filters have more room inside, there is often space for special materials that can provide biological filtration. Ceramic noodles, rings, and other shapes offer lots of surface area for nitrifying bacteria to colonize. These items can be rinsed in aquarium water without removing or killing the bacteria.

Undergravel or sponge filters provide the most efficient biological filtration, but if such units are impractical or unavailable, using an outside power filter for biological filtration will work. For very large aquariums, two or more outside power filters or canister filters can be used.

WATER TEMPERATURE AND AQUARIUM HEATERS

For the vast majority of tropical fish, a water temperature of 76 to 78 degrees Fahrenheit will be fine. Some species like cooler water and some prefer warmer water, but as a compromise, this range works well. If you are having difficulty deciding what fish to buy, it wouldn't hurt to choose fish that prefer the same temperature range. Goldfish are not tropical fish and do better at temperatures closer to 65 degrees Fahrenheit.

It is very important that the water temperature be consistent. Rapid fluctuations in temperature, particularly down, cause physical stress to fish that often leads to disease. The solution to maintaining the correct water temperature is an aquarium heater and thermostat.

Aquarium heaters are available in a variety of types, sizes, and prices. When it comes to aquarium heaters, trying to save money is not a good idea. The reliability of a heater is too crucial to risk buying an inexpensive one.

The weak link in any heater is the thermostat, which regulates the heater, turning it on and off to maintain the desired temperature. The quality of design, materials, and construction of the thermostat is one of the things that separates unreliable heaters from good ones. In cheap heaters, the thermostat often sticks—either open or closed—and this can be disastrous.

When the thermostat is stuck in the closed position, the heater remains on, raising the water temperature. Unless you make a habit of checking the temperature each day, you may not notice there is a problem until the fish have died, either directly from the heat of the water or because the warm water is unable to hold enough dissolved oxygen to support them.

Aquarium heaters

Red-tailed Anostomus

If the thermostat sticks in the open position, the heater never turns on and the water temperature begins to drop. How low the temperature will drop depends directly on the room temperature. In the summer, when the room may be in the 70- to 80-degree Fahrenheit range, the temperature may not even drop at all.

As a general rule, the more water a tank holds, the more stable the aquatic environment will be. It will take a 50-gallon tank much longer to drop in temperature than a 10-gallon tank. The same is not true for temperature increases, though, because the heater wattage is chosen to match the size of tank it will be in. The rule of thumb is five watts per gallon, which will allow the heater to raise the temperature of one gallon of water by one degree Fahrenheit in one hour. Thus, a 10-gallon tank would use a 50-watt heater and a 50-gallon tank would use a 250-watt heater. For larger tanks it is often necessary to use more than one heater to achieve the desired wattage.

In fact, using more than one heater is actually a good idea for any size aquarium in terms of safety. When two smaller heaters are used that equal the wattage of one heater, the possibility of complete heater failure is almost eliminated. If one heater should stick in the closed position, the temperature will rise only half as fast, giving you a greater

chance of catching the problem before it becomes serious. If one of the heaters sticks in the open position, the other heater will prevent the temperature from dropping as far or as rapidly.

A complete heating system must also include a thermometer so that you can monitor the temperature of the tank. Either the normal red-alcohol variety for inside the tank or one of the digital types that sticks on the outside of the glass will work. Because there is a range of accuracy among any of these thermometers, it is a good idea to look at several of them and pick one that seems to show a reading in the middle of the range or that shows the most common reading.

There are two basic heater designs. One hangs into the water from the frame of the tank and the other is completely submersible and can be placed anywhere in the aquarium, usually by using suction cups to stick it on the tank. With either design, there is always a water-line mark on the body of heater that indicates how much of the heater must be in the water for it to operate properly. The water-line mark is very important. Should the heater be plugged in without water being up to the mark, the heater could stay on and become very hot, possibly causing damage.

Artificial plants

An aquarium hood

LIGHTING AND PLANTS

Aquarium lighting makes it possible to fully appreciate the beauty of the fish and the aquascaping in the tank. It also provides necessary illumination if you choose to use live plants. Assuming the location for the tank has been chosen carefully, tank lighting will allow you to control the amount and duration of light the aquarium receives. For all these reasons, the aquarium hood, which contains the light fixture, is an essential component.

The hood fulfills several functions in addition to providing illumination for the tank. It minimizes the evaporation of tank water and it prevents dust and other items from entering the tank easily. It also stops most fish from jumping out of the tank. Some fish, however, manage to jump through even very small spaces in the hood, in places where equipment is set up. The back of most hoods contains precut openings for filters and heaters. These

openings can be pushed or cut out as needed. If they are larger than the items they are intended for, a fish may find its way through the extra space. As a general rule, this only happens if the fish is under considerable stress to begin with.

Many hoods come equipped to accept incandescent light bulbs. These can be adequate for illuminating the tank, but they do have drawbacks. Incandescent bulbs generate quite a bit of heat, only adding to the problem of keeping aquariums from overheating during the warmer months. The bulbs don't last very long and can use a lot of electricity, especially in a larger tank where several of them would be required.

For these reasons, a hood with a fluorescent fixture already installed or a kit to convert the hood to fluorescent lighting should be used. Despite their higher initial cost, there are several advantages to fluorescent tubes. They run cooler, last much longer, and use much less energy than incandescent bulbs. They are also able to supply enough light to successfully grow live plants.

Many hoods, however, do not have room for more than one fluorescent tube, which may not be enough to keep live plants. The usual recommendation for lighting is three watts of light for each gallon of water. Although inexact, this guideline is a good indicator of the minimum wattage needed. A second light fixture will often be needed. The exact requirements of your aquarium will depend on its size, the number and type of plants it has, and the number and type of fish it has. It is best to consult your regular dealer about this so you can tailor the lighting to your exact needs.

There are actually two concerns with light: intensity and duration. If there is insufficient intensity, leaving the lights on longer will not help. One sign of inadequate light is that plants will have long stems but few leaves. In a properly lit tank, the lights need only be on for eight to ten hours. It should also be noted that some fish do not like very bright light, and all fish need to have regular periods of darkness, just as they do in nature.

Live plants can add beauty to any aquarium and are good for the fish as well. Fish feel more secure when there are plants to hide in. Some fish will spawn among plants, and vegetarian species will eat plants. Because you are not likely to want your aquarium plants eaten, you will either have to avoid vegetarian species or use plastic plants instead.

Golden Barbs

A Golden Butterfly Dwarf Cichlid

Many species of live plants will do well in an aquarium, but some do better than others depending on the water chemistry and the amount of light. Do not use house plants in an aquarium. They will not last long and will contribute to water quality problems as they begin to decay. Unfortunately, some dealers are not familiar enough with live plants to always know whether the plants they carry are truly aquatic species or not. A good book on aquarium plants is very helpful in this regard and will also provide extensive information on the care and maintenance of plants.

Live plants will compete with algae for nutrients in the water and so limit their growth. Many hobbyists think algae are unattractive, but they are a natural part of any aquatic ecosystem and can provide food for some species of fish. Problems with these single-celled plants begin when they multiply too rapidly, which is usually the result of too many nutrients in the water and too much light being available. Partial water changes and a reduction in the number of hours the tank lights are on usually control excess algae. If the tank is located where it receives sunlight, it can be impossible to control algae growth.

Plastic plants are preferred by many hobbyists. They can be very realistic in appearance, and they largely eliminate the need to worry about having enough light. In addition, some species of fish are stressed by intense illumination. They can be uncomfortable in tanks with the bright lighting required for plant growth. Artificial plants make it much easier to decorate their tanks suitably.

WATER CHEMISTRY AND TEST KITS

The water you pour into the tank has several characteristics that you need to consider. These include the pH, how hard or soft it is, and any chemicals that may have been added that could endanger the fish. In addition, the fish introduce other compounds into the water that will slowly reduce the water quality. Looking at the water tells you nothing about its chemistry and very little about its quality.

Monitoring water chemistry and water quality requires test kits. It is surprising how many people will spend a substantial amount of money for an aquarium setup but balk at spending a few extra dollars for three basic test kits—ammonia, nitrite, and pH. There are actually many more types of test kits available, but these three are the minimum needed to check the water. Other kits test for nitrate, copper, chlorine, dissolved oxygen, and so on.

There are differences in test kits that you will want to take into consideration when choosing them. Some kits have liquid components, or reagents, that test the water, and others have dry reagents. As a rule, dry reagent kits have a longer shelf life and are more reliable than kits with liquid reagents. However, all test kits have a limited shelf life, so you want to buy only kits that have expiration dates for the reagents clearly marked either on the box or somewhere on the packaging inside.

You will find that some kits are easier to use than others. In particular, be aware that most kits require you to compare the color of the water sample being tested with a set of standard colors in order to judge the results of the test. Ideally, because you will be holding the vial with the test sample up to the light to see the color, the set of standard colors should also be viewed the same way. Unfortunately, most test kits use a printed color chart, which forces you to compare a sample illuminated by direct light with a chart using reflected light, which can make accurate comparison difficult.

The ammonia and nitrite test kits are the most critical. The kits are used both to monitor the rise and fall of these compounds, indicating the completion of the initial nitrogen cycle, and as a regular check on the water quality. If any of your fish become sick and upon checking the water you discover that either ammonia or nitrite is higher than it should be, you will have a clue as to the source of the problem.

Knowing the pH of your water is important, not only to have an idea of what it is but also to compare later with the tank water to judge how things are functioning in the tank. A simple test kit will provide a reasonably accurate reading of the pH.

The pH scale runs from 0 to 14, and for monitoring aquarium water, you need to work in increments of tenths. A pH value of 7 is the midpoint, which means the water is neutral. As the pH values go down from this midpoint, the water is increasingly acidic; as the value goes up from the midpoint, the water is increasingly alkaline. A change of one whole number (i.e., 7.5 to 6.5) actually represents a change in acidity or alkalinity of 100 times.

Many aquarium fish that originate from South America prefer softer, more acidic water, whereas fish from East Africa do best in hard, alkaline water. These are just two examples. Unless you intend to breed a species that is very particular about water chemistry, you will find that the stability of the pH in an aquarium is far more important than the exact value.

Large, rapid changes in pH are often fatal to fish. Any change greater than 0.2 in a 24-hour period will cause physical stress for most fish. There are products on the market that can alter the pH up or down. However, changing the pH that quickly can cause the very problems you're trying to avoid, and the chemicals provide only a temporary solution. Once you use them, it can be difficult to maintain the proper pH without them. You would also have to store a supply of water with the altered pH for regular and emergency water changes.

Most fish will do fine in a broad range of values starting as low as 6.5 and going up to 8.0. Some species will do better at even higher or lower values than these, but for all practical purposes, it is best to allow the pH to settle at a value and simply leave it there.

As a natural part of the biological processes in an aquatic environment, the pH in the tank will become increasingly acidic over time. The change is very gradual, though, and so poses no real threat to the fish. Eventually, the pH would drop low enough to cause problems, but the partial water changes you'll do as a part of regular tank maintenance will keep that from happening.

You should know if your tap water is hard or soft. Hard water has a high content of certain minerals—magnesium, calcium and iron salts—and soft water does not. The biggest concern with tap water, though, is what the city water department puts in it. Most municipal water companies add chlorine or chloramine to the water to kill certain bacteria that are harmful to people. Unfortunately, these chemicals are themselves harmful to fish and must be removed from the water.

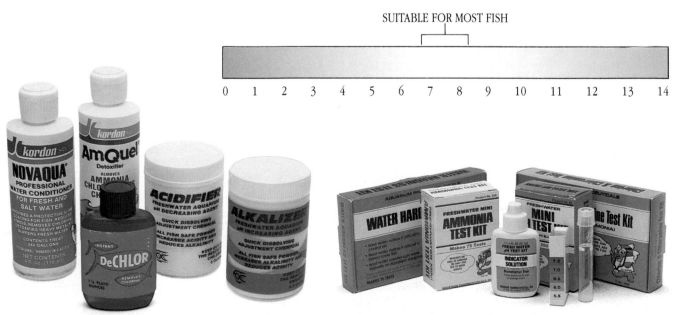

SUITABLE FOR MOST FISH

0 1 2 3 4 5 6 7 8 9 10 11 12 13 14

Left: *Water conditioners* Right: *Test kits*

Every pet store has a selection of chemicals that will easily dechlorinate the water. For dealing with chloramine, however, you need something a little different. Chloramine is a combination of chlorine and ammonia. When a normal dechlorinator is used at double the recommended amount, it will break the bond between these two compounds, neutralizing the chlorine but releasing the ammonia. The added ammonia may be more than the nitrifying bacteria in your tank's biological filter can handle. The only way to handle this problem is to use a one-step water conditioner designed to handle chloramine. This product will break the bond between chlorine and ammonia and neutralize both.

The easiest way to determine what your local water company is adding to the water is to call them and ask. Be aware, however, that cities using chlorine may suddenly switch to chloramine, which could cause problems if your tank doesn't have effective biological filtration or is overcrowded.

If you have well water, you might consider having it checked by a professional laboratory. Although there will be no chlorine or chloramine in the water, it may contain high levels of iron or other substances that could prove harmful to your fish. In areas with farming, well water sometimes contains high levels of nitrates, which only add to the levels already in the tank from the nitrogen cycle. These nitrates come from the fertilizers used on farm crops.

AQUASCAPING

The first consideration when decorating an aquarium is the gravel. The size of the individual pieces of gravel is particularly important if the tank has an undergravel filter. If the gravel is too large, there won't be as much total surface area for the nitrifying bacteria. On the other hand, if the gravel is too small, it will clog with particles easily and restrict the flow of water through the gravel bed. The best gravel sizes are #2 or #3, which are two and three millimeters in diameter respectively.

Although the color of gravel is a matter of personal choice, neutral colors are more natural and do not compete with the fish for attention. They also help to make the fish more comfortable. You may notice that many fish are dark on top and lighter on the bottom. This is a form of camouflage called countershading. The fish will be less visible to predators when viewed from above against the dark bottom of a stream or pond, or when viewed from below against the light color of the sky. For this reason, fish feel more secure over dark gravel.

Aquarium gravel

Cured driftwood

Aquascaping rocks

Hiding places are an important part of aquascaping.

While you are contouring the gravel, you can use rocks and cured pieces of driftwood to create terraces, ledges, and caves. These will add visual interest while providing shelter and hiding places for the fish. Choose rocks that are not going to alter the chemistry of the water. Your local aquarium store will have a good selection of rocks that are safe for the tank, along with driftwood that has been properly cured. Curing driftwood yourself is a slow, tedious task. Incompletely cured driftwood can pollute the water and kill the fish.

Do not use corals and shells for decorations. These items not only look out of place in a freshwater aquarium but they can also make the water harder and more alkaline than it normally would be. Also, avoid rocks that have rough surfaces or sharp edges that could injure the fish. It is very important that all rockwork be stable. The base of any large rocks should rest securely on the tank bottom, not on the surface of the gravel bed. Should the rocks fall, the aquarium glass could crack or fish could be injured.

Aquascaping decorations

OTHER ITEMS

There is a large variety of basic items and accessories available for aquarists to choose from, but only some are absolutely necessary. You will want to have enough air line tubing to run between the air pump and the air stones, as well as some extra air stones. Over time, air stones begin to clog, which reduces their efficiency and causes unnecessary wear on the air pump.

You should also have an extra set of replacement diaphragms on hand for the air pump. If not, your dealer can replace them for you when they wear out. Some hobbyists like to be prepared for larger problems. If you are willing to make the investment, a back-up pump and even an extra heater or filter are insurance against equipment failure.

A gang valve is very useful for distributing and regulating air flow. Air from the pump goes first to the gang valve and then separately to each air stone. The air stones can then be regulated individually, and if the pump puts out more air than you need, excess air can be routed through an unused valve. Routing the surplus air through an air stone reduces any noise coming from this line. Bleeding off excess air keeps the diaphragms in the pump from wearing out too quickly.

A Zebra Danio

Gang valves

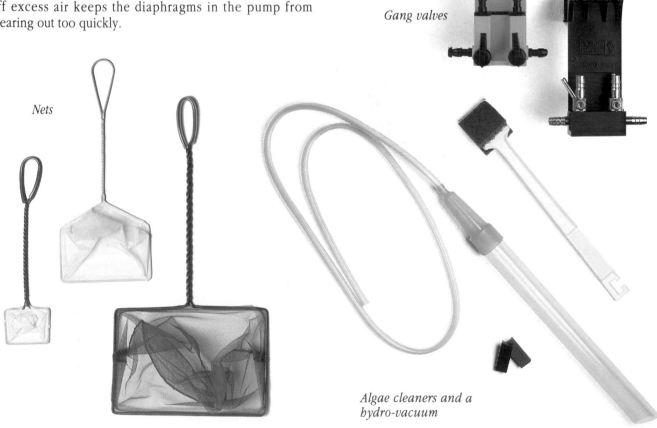

Nets

Algae cleaners and a hydro-vacuum

Angelfish

If the air pump is going to sit on the floor or on a shelf that is below the water line in the tank, a one-way check valve should be used in the line between the pump and the gang valve. Should the electricity go off and the diaphragms stop in the wrong position, water could be siphoned from the tank through the air lines into the pump, ruining it. A check valve will prevent the water from reaching the pump. If the pump has more than one outlet, there should be a check valve for each line.

You can use several different items for keeping the inside of the front glass free from algae. A sponge or plastic pad on a long handle, a pair of magnets—one with a cleaning pad and the other with a felt pad—or a long-handled plastic scraper will make it easy to remove algae.

A good-quality, one-step water conditioner should always be available for regular water changes as well as any emergencies, such as having to set up a hospital tank for a sick fish. A supply of mechanical filtering material and granular activated carbon should be on hand for regular maintenance. If the filter uses special seals or O-rings, an extra set of these should be kept available.

Buy at least two nets. It is easier to catch fish in the tank by using one net to guide or force the fish toward the second net, and it's also a good deal less stressful for the fish.

One of the best investments you can make is to purchase a hydro-vacuum to help with tank maintenance. These gravel cleaners are inexpensive, but they're an essential tool for keeping the tank clean and healthy. This device will be explained in detail in the section on aquarium maintenance.

Finally, you will need a bucket or two, paper towels, and glass cleaner. There are many other accessories that you can buy, but it is better to get the tank up and running for a while first. Then you will be able to determine which, if any, of these other items you would find useful.

CHAPTER 3

Setup and Maintenance

Setting up your aquarium should be a relatively simple procedure. You should be able to get the whole system up and running in a couple of hours at the most, although you'll have to wait some time before you add the fish. The most important thing for you to do before you begin is to be sure you're prepared. Know in detail what you want the aquarium to be like when you're done, and be sure you have all the equipment, space, and tools you'll need.

A pair of Black Phantom Tetras

A new, brand-name tank will almost certainly not leak, but you may want to be absolutely sure about this before setting up the tank in its final location. Choose a dry area, cover it with newspapers, and place the tank on them. Very carefully fill the tank to the rim with cool water and wait for an hour or two. If the newspapers are wet, you know you have a problem with your tank.

If there are no leaks, empty the tank, wipe out the interior, and place it on the aquarium stand in its permanent location. If you like, you can apply a background material to the back of the tank. This is optional, but many fish feel more secure if the back and sides are covered. Once this is done, you are ready to install the filtration system.

The undergravel filter plate should be rinsed thoroughly and then placed in the tank. If the plate does not fit the bottom exactly, place it so that it is up against the back of the tank and centered.

The lift tubes can be installed next. Because the tubes are designed to fit the tallest tanks, you may need to cut them to fit your particular aquarium. If so, cut the tubes so that the top will be just below the surface of the water when the tank is filled.

Next, you must hook up all of the air line tubing to the undergravel filter and any air stones. Connect a length of tubing to the air pump. If you are using a check valve to ensure that no water can flow into the air pump, make sure it is facing the correct direction. There is often an arrow on the body of the valve indicating this. You can also test the valve by blowing into either end to determine which way it allows air to flow. Cut lengths of air tubing to go from the check valve to the gang valve or directly to the air line stems at the top of the undergravel lift tubes. Even if your air pump has two outlets and you are only using two lift tube air stones, a gang valve offers better control of the air flow to each piece of equipment. When using a gang valve, the lines going to it from the air pump are connected at the side of the valve, and the lines going from the gang valve to the tank are connected at the top of the valve. Make sure that there is a small amount of slack in the air tubing to avoid kinking the lines and blocking the

A Dwarf Gourami

flow of air. The air line going to the lift tubes or to any air stones in the tank should run through the appropriate openings in the back of the tank hood.

If you are using powerheads instead of an air pump to create water flow through the lift tubes, the lift tube should go into the opening in the plate that is one over from the corner opening. In this situation, the lift tubes can't go in the corner openings because powerheads won't fit into the corners of the tank after the hood is installed. All other openings in the undergravel filter should be closed with the caps provided with the filter. For undergravel filters with just one plate, only one powerhead is usually necessary.

The mechanical filtration system is next. You have a great variety of filters to choose from, and each has its own particular requirements for preparation. Some may need assembly and others may not. Read the instructions that came with the filter and follow them carefully. If you still have trouble fitting everything together, check with your dealer. This is part of the service that the store you bought the filter from should offer. Set the filter up but don't plug it in yet.

Set up the temperature control system for your tank. As with the mechanical filters, you have many heaters and thermometers to choose from. Follow the specific instructions provided with your equipment. Put everything in place but don't plug the heater in yet.

With the filters in place and the thermometer set up, you are now ready to begin aquascaping. For biological filtration, an inch of gravel would be adequate, but for stability

and aesthetics, two to three inches is better. As an estimate, two pounds of gravel per gallon of water is probably the minimum amount to purchase. All gravel should be rinsed in small quantities in a bucket under running water before it goes into the aquarium. Stir the gravel in the bucket and continue rinsing until the water is no longer cloudy and has no solid matter floating in it.

As you add gravel to the tank, you want to place more toward the back so that when you are finished, the gravel slopes down to the front of the tank. The visual effect of the sloping tends to make the tank look deeper. Also, the slope will tend to cause the various bits and pieces of organic matter that accumulate on the gravel to work their way to the front of the tank, where they can be more easily removed. The slope will also even the flow of water through the undergravel filter. The lift tube that draws the water through the filter plate is at the back of the tank, so it has less of an effect on the water at the front of the tank. If the gravel at the front isn't as deep, though, it creates less resistance for the water to overcome, and the flow of water through the gravel will be roughly the same near the lift tube as it is away from the lift tube.

After the gravel has been laid down, you can add any other aquascaping materials. Remember to think about the arrangement. You're creating a terrain of sorts for your fish, and you must consider them. They'll want caves and crevices for hiding, and any territorial species will want bounded areas they can claim as their own. Also remember that you should like the way it looks. The backdrop you're creating can have a big impact on the aquarium's overall look, so it pays to get it right. Don't add any plants yet; they go in after the tank has been partially filled.

It's finally time to add some water, but don't fill the tank just yet. Add only enough water to make it about two thirds of the way full and use lukewarm water from the tap. Don't use hot water, which can crack the glass. Cold water is no problem, but it can take quite a while for the aquarium heater to bring it to the correct temperature. Another option is to use a high-quality kitchen thermometer and mix the hot and cold water until it reaches the desired temperature.

To avoid disturbing the aquascaping, the flow of water into the tank should be eased somehow. One method is to lay newspapers over the aquascaping, pour the water on the papers, and then remove them. You can also place a bowl or cup on the gravel and pour the water into that. A third possibility is to place one of your hands palm up in the

Starting It Up

1. *Position the undergravel filter plate in the bottom of the tank.*

2. *Install the lift tubes along with their air stones and air line tubing.*

3. *Begin to set up the air pump. Attach a length of air line tubing and a one-way check valve to the pump.*

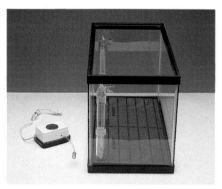

4. *Run a length of tubing from the check valve to a gang valve, and position the gang valve on the tank.*

5. *Run tubing from the gang valve to each of the lift tubes.*

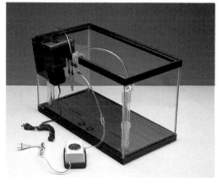

6. *Install the mechanical filtration unit. Carefully follow any assembly or installation instructions from the manufacturer.*

7. *Install the heater/thermostat unit. Again, carefully follow any instructions from the manufacturer.*

8. *Rinse the gravel thoroughly before adding it to the tank. Put more gravel in the rear of the tank, creating a gentle downward slope from back to front.*

9. *Add rockwork, driftwood, or any other large aquascaping material. Push them firmly into the gravel bed and build up a little gravel around their bases to position them securely.*

10. *Fill the tank two-thirds full with water. Make the water as close as possible to the desired temperature of the aquarium, and pour it carefully so the aquascaping is not disturbed.*

11. *Add plants to the tank. Proper positioning can help to make the equipment less obvious. Fill the tank the rest of the way with water.*

12. *Add the thermometer. Turn on the equipment, one piece at a time, and make any necessary adjustments.*

tank just above the gravel and pour the water onto your hand. You can also use one of the bulkier, more stable pieces of aquascaping—a rock, for instance—to break the flow of the water.

With the tank two-thirds full of water, the live or plastic plants can go in. Tall plants will look best in the back, and you can use them to hide the lift tubes, heater, air tubing, and other equipment. Smaller plants can go on the sides and near the front of the tank. Clustering plants around rockwork often creates a nice effect.

Do not mix species of plants so that they are scattered throughout the tank. In nature, plants of the same species grow in groups, and you want to duplicate this effect in the tank. Plants of the same species growing together are also often of different sizes, representing a mixture of young plants and mature plants.

The tank now has everything in it except the fish, and you can add the rest of the water. Add enough so that the water line will be hidden by the hood. The water you're adding should be about the same temperature as the water already in the tank. After the tank is completely filled, you can begin turning on the equipment.

With all of the valves of the gang valve completely open, turn on the air pump. Air bubbles should be flowing from all air stones. Adjust the gang valve to even out the air flow. It is very important that the bubbles flow equally from all lift tubes, if you have more than one. If the flow is greater in some tubes than in others, the undergravel filter may not work correctly because the tubes with the strongest flow can actually pull water down the tubes with the weakest flow.

Once the undergravel filter is operating properly, the power filter can be started. The filter box or canister must be at least half full of water in order to prime the filter. The body of some filters is marked where the water level should be. Plug the filter in. The filter will fill with water to its normal operating level while any air in the system is expelled. After this has happened, the filter should run smoothly.

The heater can be plugged in now. When the water temperature of the tank is already at or very close to where it should be, setting the thermostat is easy. When the thermometer says that the water temperature is in the proper range, adjust the heater control until the heater's indicator light comes on. Then, turn the knob the other way just enough for the light to go out. Over the next day or so, check two or three times to see if the heater is maintaining the temperature as it should be. It may take a couple of days to get the heating unit set at the correct level.

Add enough water conditioner for the volume of water in the tank. The hood can be closed and the light turned on. Clean the glass and then stand back and admire your work.

Let the tank run for at least a day and keep an eye on things. Check the temperature and note that the filters are operating properly. Don't be surprised if the water becomes cloudy on the second day. This is most likely the result of bacteria responding to light and warmth. It will clear up in a few days.

Only when you are sure that the tank is running properly and will be a healthy aquatic home should you actually go shopping for your first fish. While you wait, spend some time learning as much about aquarium fish as you can.

A Swordtail pair: female above and male below

AQUARIUM MAINTENANCE

The amount of aquarium maintenance you have to do is directly related to how closely you follow the three basic rules of fishkeeping. If the tank is overcrowded, if you consistently feed the fish too much food, and if you seldom do partial water changes, the filter system will be unable to keep the water quality where it should be. If you find yourself dealing with diseased and dying fish on a regular basis, you are almost certainly doing at least one of these three things wrong.

Aquarium maintenance is not time consuming if the tank is set up correctly and you go about it properly. You should get in the habit of looking at the fish closely every day or two, as well as checking the water temperature. Once each week, clean the inside of the front glass (and the side glass if you want), change 10 or 15 percent of the water, and clean the outside of the glass. You could do this every 10 days, but it is usually easier to remember if you perform maintenance on the same day each week.

If the tank is lightly stocked and you are careful about not overfeeding, this basic maintenance can be done every other week. Undercrowding also means that more extensive maintenance, particularly on the filter, doesn't have to be done as often either. If you keep large fish that consume greater amounts of food and thus produce more waste products, you may have to change as much as 50 percent of the water each time. Note that tank size makes a difference, too. Not only are larger tanks a more stable aquatic environment for the fish, but they also require less work than smaller aquariums.

When doing water changes, be sure to use what may be the most important accessory you can own: a hydro-vacuum. Essentially, the hydro-vacuum consists of a hose to siphon the water from the tank with a special attachment on the end that goes into the tank. The attachment is a long, clear tube that is much wider than the siphon hose.

To use a hydro-vacuum, push the attachment into the gravel and suck on the other end of the hose to get the water started. Make sure you hold the outer end of the hose lower than the rim of the tank. As soon as you see the water in the hose cross over the top of the tank, place the end of the hose in a bucket positioned below the water level. You will see the gravel swirl around in the large end of the hydro-vacuum, releasing clouds of waste material that will be drawn out of the tank along with the siphoned water. By pulling the attachment out of the gravel and pushing it into the gravel nearby, you will be able to effectively clean the gravel bed without removing the gravel from the tank.

Feeling that this activity will disturb the nitrifying bacteria in the gravel, some hobbyists vacuum only half of the gravel bed with each water change, alternating from one side to the other each time. Cleaning the gravel really shouldn't have any ill effects on the bacteria, though, so this caution is probably not necessary.

Every two to eight weeks, depending on how the tank is managed and what sort of fish it houses, the filter materials in the power filter will need to be changed. If the mechanical filter material is reusable, place it in a bucket with some aquarium water and squeeze it a few times to clean it or simply rinse it with tap water. If you use tap water, make sure it is the same temperature as the tank water. If you are using some type of bio-media in the power filter, follow the same procedure as for the mechanical filter material.

The granular activated carbon will have to be replaced. Once the carbon is saturated with molecules it can't adsorb any more. Some hobbyists test the carbon by tinting the water very lightly with a harmless food dye. If the dye is removed by the carbon, it does not need to be replaced. It is easier to simply use new carbon when cleaning or changing the mechanical filter material.

This is all the maintenance an aquarium should require. Do not tear the tank down, clean everything thoroughly, and then set it up again. This only destroys all of the beneficial bacteria in the aquarium, forcing you to break in the tank again. If an aquarium requires that kind of cleaning, there are severe overcrowding or maintenance problems that need to be dealt with.

CHAPTER 4

Selecting and Caring for the Fish

New hobbyists who have had problems keeping fish alive for even a few months are always shocked to find out that the normal life span of the typical aquarium fish is measured not in months but in years. Although it varies from species to species, aquarium fish should live anywhere from three to seven years, or longer. Goldfish can live for 20 years or more. Fish can actually live longer, healthier lives and sometimes even grow larger in an aquarium than they do in the wild.

In nature, a fish's food supplies can come and go with the changing of the seasons and unusual weather patterns. The amount of food may be limited, and it can take a lot of energy to find enough to survive. Predators, including other fish, will keep nearly all the young of any species from reaching adulthood. Few fish get to die of old age in the wild. Fish that are too weak or slow will quickly become dinner. Although aquariums have limitations, they can be an environment where fish are able to flourish.

A shoal of Tiger Barbs

FEEDING THE FISH

One of the three rules of fishkeeping is to not overfeed the fish. All uneaten food in a tank quickly pollutes the water. Overfeeding kills the fish with kindness. The best guideline is to feed only enough food each time so that the fish finish it within five minutes.

Most fish will do well on a diet consisting primarily of dry flake food. Use only brand-name, high-quality food. There is a wide variety of flake foods, and it is best to purchase several kinds and feed a different one each time. This helps ensure a more balanced diet for the fish. Larger fish and many catfish will do better on pellet foods, which have more bulk. Freeze-dried foods are particularly good for fish that need a lot of protein. By occasionally offering fresh-frozen or live foods, you will ensure that your fish are getting a nutritionally complete diet.

A variety of fish foods

When shopping for food, remember that commercial foods have a limited shelf life. If the containers are dusty or look like they have been on the shelf a long time, go somewhere else. Purchase small containers. Yes, it is more economical to buy larger sizes, but once the containers are opened, the nutritional value of the food will begin to deteriorate. Within three to six months, less than half the

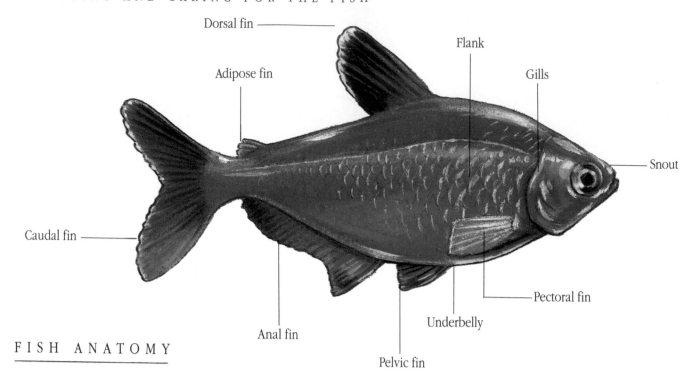

Dorsal fin

Adipose fin

Flank

Gills

Snout

Caudal fin

Pectoral fin

Underbelly

Anal fin

Pelvic fin

FISH ANATOMY

original nutritional value remains. For this reason, do not buy bulk-packed flake foods unless you have enough fish to consume it within a few months.

For vegetarian fish, there are flake foods that are formulated to provide much more vegetable material and less protein. Flake foods can be supplemented with freeze-dried, frozen, and even live foods, all of which are available at the aquarium store.

Many hobbyists keep small catfish in their tanks to eat excess food that falls to the bottom of the tank. These fish must receive the same quantity and quality of food as the rest of the residents. Because they feed at the bottom of the tank, it is best to feed them just before turning off the tank lights. The catfish will feed in the dark while the other fish are resting. Heavy pellet foods sink and work especially well for this purpose.

Healthy fish can go for at least one or two weeks without eating. When you leave on vacation for a week or so, don't worry about not feeding the fish. More fish have probably died from severe water pollution as a result of well-meaning friends or neighbors overfeeding the fish than ever suffered from not eating for a week.

DISEASE
Diagnosing and treating fish diseases is so complex that entire books have been written on the subject. Fish can contract a great many illnesses, and curing them can take a great deal of knowledge and effort. In addition, preventing disease is almost always easier than curing it.

Fish that live in good quality water, receive a balanced diet, and do not continually suffer from physical stress seldom get sick. Their immune systems are quite capable of protecting them from disease-causing organisms, which are always in the water. When they do get sick, though, it always helps to notice their condition early. As a general rule, changes in the physical appearance and behavior of the fish are indicators of other problems, so it pays to observe your fish carefully. If things look suspicious, test the water to make sure there are no problems there. As a precaution, clean the filter and change a third of the water in the tank.

When you suspect that any of the fish may be sick, *do not* add any medications to the tank. You should not treat the tank without knowing what the fish is suffering from. Many fish medications are ineffective or contain so little medication that they do no good at all. Antibiotics in particular are a problem. If used in small amounts, the bacteria they are supposed to kill can develop resistance to the drugs. When used at much higher doses, the nitrifying bacteria in the biological filter can be wiped out. Most medications include instructions to change some of the water before each dose. As often as not, it is the water changes, not the medication, that are responsible for the fish getting better.

One common but easily cured disease is ich, which is caused by a parasite, *Ichthyophthirius multifillis*. This disease is typically brought on by physical stress, such as the fish being handled or the temperature of the water changing rapidly. The fish's body and fins will be covered with very small white spots. Fortunately, ich can be cured easily

40

by raising the water temperature to about 84 degrees Fahrenheit and treating with the proper medication. Avoid medications with copper in them. Copper can build up in an aquarium and then suddenly be released if the water chemistry changes, killing the fish. Copper is particularly dangerous in tanks with soft water.

Another common disease is fin rot. This disease results in the edges of the fins taking on an uneven appearance as they get shorter and shorter. This disease, which often results from poor environmental conditions, is easily treated with many of the medications available just for this purpose.

One other somewhat common disease is fungus—typically a fuzzy, white cottony patch. This is a secondary disease, taking hold at the site of a physical injury. If the water quality is poor, fungus can infiltrate the wound. This problem is also easily cured with the proper medication. Ask your dealer for advice.

CHOOSING THE FISH

A visit to any large aquarium or pet store will reveal an astonishing variety of fish—a couple hundred species or more. Of these many possibilities, only some are suitable for new aquarists. Never purchase fish without knowing enough about them to determine how well they are likely to do in your particular aquarium. Often, hobbyists find themselves leaving a pet store with a fish that they just couldn't pass up without having any idea what it eats, how large it gets, or if it has any unusual care requirements. While it is always fun to acquire a new fish, doing it haphazardly can be disastrous and costly.

When choosing fish, there are a number of factors to consider. For example, fish that are found only in very specific habitat conditions are not going to do as well in an aquarium that differs much from their natural environment. Species that have adapted to a wide variety of conditions in nature tend to be the hardiest fish in an aquarium. Fish that are hardy are more likely to survive most aquarium conditions.

Your fish also need to be compatible with each other. Just about every new aquarist starts out by keeping a community aquarium containing a variety of fish that differ in size, shape, and color. Often, the fish in such a tank originate from different parts of the world and have adapted to different water conditions. Their behavior patterns and food preferences may also differ. This means that even if all of the fish are hardy, if they are not compatible, there will be difficulties. Compatibility is essential to success with a community setting.

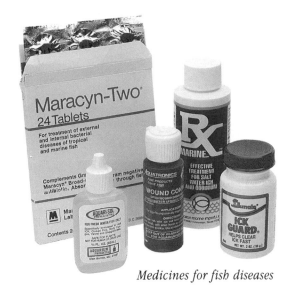

Medicines for fish diseases

Compatibility is generally assumed to mean that the fish get along. In other words, the fish are peaceful and do not harass one another. Fish that are subjected to harassment on a continual basis are under so much physical stress that they are far more likely to become sick, no matter how good the water quality is. As important as this basic compatibility is, however, your fish need to be compatible in other ways too.

If the fish prefer very different water conditions—some doing best in hard, alkaline water and others doing better in soft, acid water—you will not be able to provide the best environment for all of them. The fish least compatible with your aquarium water chemistry may not grow as large or exhibit their best color.

Behavior patterns are also important. Fast-swimming fish will disturb and upset fish that swim slowly. Fish that are aggressive swimmers will often take more than their fair share of food at feeding time. The more timid species will hold back and thus get little to eat. Adding more food to compensate only increases the problem of uneaten food in the tank, making it more difficult to maintain good water quality.

Behavior differences can be very disruptive. Even when fish have peaceful dispositions, conflicts can still come up among them in the tank. Fish that are territorial will keep other species from entering their area, limiting the amount of space for all the others. If there aren't enough hiding places, more dominant fish will maintain control of the few that do exist in the tank.

Fish that have different food requirements can make it difficult to supply each species with the appropriate diet. Those that require lots of protein will need different foods than those that require more vegetable matter. Growth and

Cardinal Tetras and Platy

Also remember that the vast majority of fish sold in stores are very young. You must stock the tank based on the normal adult size that the fish should reach when mature. This will mean that for the first several months, the tank will appear somewhat empty. Don't fill that space with more fish! The small fish already in the tank can only grow to healthy adult size if there is room.

Healthy fish are active. Avoid fish that have poor color, fins clamped close to the body, or odd swimming behavior. When you approach the tank, the fish should crowd to the front in anticipation of being fed. If some of the fish in the tank are clearly sick, do not purchase any fish from that tank.

When choosing fish, keep in mind that you don't want to select ones that all live in the same part of the tank. That is, you want a community in which some fish swim near the top of the tank, others in the middle, and some at the bottom. Some species tend to stay at one level most of the time, whereas others are all over the tank.

You should try to set aside time to make a special trip to the aquarium store when you buy your fish. If you intend to do other errands besides shopping for fish, save the aquarium store for last. The bags of fish should be taken directly home. The small volume of water in each bag is subject to rapid temperature changes and is easily polluted, and the fish will be under considerable stress.

It has been common advice for years to float the bags in the aquarium for at least 15 minutes to equalize the temperatures of the bags with the tank water. However, because this only increases the stress on the fish, which are already under considerable stress from being netted, bagged, and transported, it is usually better to add the fish as soon as you arrive home. The only exception is if the water in the aquarium is colder than that in the bags, in which case floating the bags will be necessary.

Some experienced hobbyists do not add the bag water to their tank to avoid the possibility of inadvertently introducing any disease-causing organisms to the aquarium. Instead, they place a large net over a bucket and pour the contents of the bag into it, and then they release the netted fish into the aquarium. Repeat this procedure for each bag and discard the water in the bucket.

Give the fish time to adjust to their new home. The tank lights should remain off for at least several hours. Some

health are tied directly to a nutritionally balanced diet, and the proper balance can vary from one species of fish to another.

Keeping fish of vastly different sizes in the same tank, no matter how peaceful, is an invitation to disaster. Fish will eat whatever fits in their mouth. Many a novice has been shocked to discover that the angelfish and tetras that co-existed so well when they were small are no longer safe together—the increasingly larger angels have no qualms about consuming the smaller tetras.

Reading as much as you can about aquarium fish and asking your dealer for advice will help you choose the best combination of fish for your size tank. Keep in mind that descriptions of fish behavior are generalizations, and some individual fish are exceptions to the rules.

When shopping for fish, the first thing to keep in mind is that the dealer's tanks are greatly overstocked. The store tanks receive much more maintenance than home aquariums do, and the fish will only be in those tanks for a relatively short time, perhaps a week or less in many cases.

species are more prone to hiding than others, but as they become used to their surroundings they will spend more and more time in the open.

Ideally, when adding new fish to an existing tank, the new fish should spend a minimum of two weeks in a quarantine tank. This gives you time to see if they develop any diseases as a result of the stresses involved in getting them home. If you have a sponge filter in the display tank, you can transfer it to the quarantine tank and have instant biological filtration. A heater and a hood with a light are the only other requirements. The quarantine tank does not have to have gravel or aquascaping, but hiding places should be provided. Small, clean flowerpots broken in half and laid on their sides are excellent for this purpose. You should also feed established residents just before you finally add the new fish to a community tank. A full stomach will make them less aggressive.

Different fish tend to occupy different levels in an aquarium. Taking advantage of this behavior allows a more efficient use of available space.

Upper Level

Middle Level

Lower Level

CHAPTER 5

Freshwater Aquarium Fish

The fish presented in the following pages are certainly not the only species that would do well in the typical aquarium setup of a new hobbyist. They are, however, representative of the type of fish that beginning aquarists have the most success with. They are all hardy, they can thrive on common fish foods, they are suitable for community tanks, and they are widely available in aquarium stores. You may be interested in some particular species that don't appear in this book. Before purchasing any such fish, you need to find out more about them and whether or not they will be good additions to your tank. As always, consult your dealer about this.

PENGUIN FISH

Thayeria obliqua

This quiet community fish grows to two inches and does well with other fish that are small and peaceful. The water temperature should be between 72 and 82 degrees Fahrenheit. Soft to moderately hard water is fine, with a pH of 5.8 to 7.5. This species will not do well if the water quality begins to deteriorate. It eats all flake and freeze-dried foods.

This South American species inhabits several river systems of Brazil. The female tends to be larger and has a fuller body.

CARDINAL TETRA

Paracheirodon axelrodi

One of the most popular of all tropical fish, the Cardinal Tetra grows to about 1.5 inches and must be kept in shoals. Tankmates must be peaceful and not too large. A water temperature of 72 to 82 degrees Fahrenheit with a pH between 5.3 and 7.8 is good. It does well on flake and freeze-dried foods.

With its colorless fins and deep red body split by a bold blue stripe, the Cardinal makes quite a sight in an aquarium. Dark gravel and background help to emphasize the colors of this fish, and it shows its colors best in relatively soft, acidic water.

NEON TETRA

Paracheirodon innesi

Neons are very similar to Cardinal Tetras but have been available to hobbyists for a good while longer. Perhaps the most popular of all aquarium fish, Neons grow to a little over an inch in length. As with the Cardinal Tetra, a dark tank with subdued lighting enhances the colors of these fish. They can be kept in a water temperature of 68 to 78 degrees Fahrenheit at a pH of 5.5 to 8.0. Although soft water is best, they will do well in moderately hard water as long as the water quality is very good. They should be kept in shoals with other small, peaceful species, and they take all flake and freeze-dried foods.

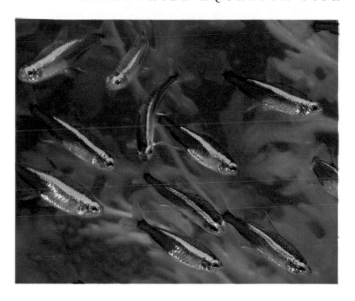

GLOWLIGHT TETRA

Hemigrammus erythrozonus

Another schooling fish, this species grows to about two inches and can be kept with other fish of similar size and temperament. Dark tank aquascaping shows off this species at its best. A water temperature in the 74 to 82 degrees Fahrenheit range with a pH of 5.8 to 7.5 and moderately soft to mildly hard water are fine. This fish is not fussy about foods, taking flake and freeze-dried varieties.

The common name comes from the obvious iridescent red stripe down the fish's side. The stripe also has a faint golden shadow along the top, which stands out in good light. Males are just a bit slimmer than females, but the difference is slight and doesn't really serve as a useful way to distinguish between them.

HEAD AND TAIL LIGHT TETRA

Hemigrammus ocellifer

This species grows to about two inches in length and does best in shoals. Colors are more intense with dark gravel and background. As long as the water temperature is between 74 and 82 degrees Fahrenheit and the pH is in the range of 5.5 to 7.0, with moderately soft to mildly hard water, it will do well. This fish does fine on flake and freeze-dried foods, but it benefits from the occasional feeding of live brine shrimp, as do all tetras.

Females are just a bit larger than the males and have a fuller, deeper underbelly. These fish are also sometimes referred to as Beaconfish.

BLACK TETRA
Gymnocorymbus ternetzi

Growing to approximately two inches in length, this fish can be kept in small groups but looks best in a large shoal. Adults are not as black in coloration as younger fish and are more prone to act aggressively toward smaller tankmates. The water temperature should be in the range of 72 to 82 degrees Fahrenheit with a pH between 5.8 and 8.2 and soft to moderately hard water. This species eats all flake and freeze-dried foods.

The natural habitat of the Black Tetra is calm South American waters with overhanging vegetation that blocks sunlight. It feeds near the surface waters, largely on insects that fall on the water's surface.

X-RAY TETRA
Pristella maxillaria

An excellent choice for beginners, this species grows to 1.5 inches. It is faster swimming than some of the other tetras and should be kept in a shoal. The water temperature can be between 72 and 82 degrees Fahrenheit. A pH from 6.0 to 8.0 is fine, as is soft to relatively hard water. All flake and freeze-dried foods are suitable.

The body coloring of this fish is unremarkable, but the fins make it rather distinctive. The tail is an off red, and the dorsal and anal fins have an unusual three-color pattern: bright yellow, black, and white.

BLACK NEON TETRA
Hyphessobrycon herbertaxelrodi

This is another peaceful species that does best in groups. It grows to 1.5 inches and can be kept with other tetras in a darkish tank with lots of plants. All tetras feel more secure and are more likely to swim in the open in well-planted tanks. A water temperature of 72 to 78 degrees Fahrenheit with a pH of 5.5 to 7.5 and soft to moderately soft water are fine. This species will eat all flake and freeze-dried foods but should also receive occasional feedings of live brine shrimp.

BLEEDING HEART TETRA
Hyphessobrycon erythrostigma

These are deep-bodied tetras that grow to two inches and must be kept in groups. They should be maintained only with other peaceful fish, including angelfish. This species does well as long as the water temperature is in the range of 75 to 82 degrees Fahrenheit with a pH of 5.6 to 7.2 and soft to mildly hard water. They will thrive on flake and freeze-dried foods and an occasional feeding of live brine shrimp.

The common name comes from the blood-red splotch on the fish's side just behind the gills. The males have an interesting dorsal fin; it's large and sharply swept back. These fish tend to be rather skittish, and you may see them swim frantically to and fro on occasion.

BLOODFIN TETRA
Aphyocharax anisitsi

The Bloodfin is an excellent community species that grows to approximately two inches in length. Like most tetras, they are most comfortable in a group of six or more. A water temperature from 68 to 78 degrees Fahrenheit is fine, but the fish show better color at the higher end of the range. They are not fussy about water chemistry, doing well with a pH of 6.0 to 8.0 in soft to relatively hard water. They will eat all flake and freeze-dried foods.

In the wild, Bloodfins normally feed on tiny invertebrates found in surface waters. The female is the larger of the species. Although normally quite docile, they become rather active during courtship, sometimes even leaping out of the water.

BLACK PHANTOM TETRA
Megalamphodus melanopterus

This tetra grows to two inches. It is a hardy species that does well in both small and large groups. A temperature in the range of 72 to 82 degrees Fahrenheit, at a pH of 5.5 to 7.5, and water that is moderately soft to slightly hard are suitable for this species. All flake and freeze-dried foods are acceptable, but regular offerings of live brine shrimp should be included in its diet.

Females are more brightly colored and have red fins. The males will sometimes visually threaten each other by facing off and spreading out their fins.

DIAMOND TETRA
Moenkhausia pitteri

A somewhat larger tetra, this species reaches 2.5 inches and exhibits intense coloration when kept in a darkly aquascaped tank. It should also have adequate swimming room in the tank. This fish should be kept at a water temperature between 74 and 82 degrees Fahrenheit with a pH between 5.5 and 7.5 and soft to moderately hard water. Flake and freeze-dried foods supplemented with live brine shrimp fulfill its dietary needs. The Diamond Tetra has violet-hued scales with a fine scattering of green and gold that creates a pleasant sparkling effect.

RED-EYE TETRA
Moenkhausia sanctaefilomenae

This is another of the larger tetras, growing to 2.5 inches. It is an undemanding species as long as the water quality is good and there is room for a group to swim actively in the tank. The Red-Eye is a fin-nipper, though; keep it with short-finned companions that are the same size or a bit larger. It does well at a water temperature in the range of 68 to 78 degrees Fahrenheit, a pH between 5.5 and 8.5, and soft to relatively hard water. Flake and freeze-dried foods are fine, although an occasional feeding of live brine shrimp is recommended.

CONGO TETRA
Phenacogrammus interruptus

Unlike all the other tetras in this section, which are from South America, this species is from Africa. It grows to 3.5 inches and should be kept in a shoal in a spacious aquarium. The Congo is a jumper and requires a tightly covered tank. Aquascaping should provide shelter from bright tank lights. Exceptionally good water quality is important. A water temperature between 74 and 82 degrees Fahrenheit, a pH of 6.0 to 6.5, and moderately soft to slightly hard water are recommended. Although flake and dried foods are a good basic diet, live brine shrimp should be a regular addition.

DWARF PENCILFISH
Nannostomus marginatus

This species, which grows to one inch, can be kept in a shoal even in a small aquarium. A water temperature between 74 and 82 degrees Fahrenheit, a pH of 5.8 to 7.5, and moderately soft to slightly hard water are suitable. Small flake and freeze-dried foods should be provided with supplements of live brine shrimp. This small South American fish has a striking color pattern, with a bold red stripe on the side and red splotches on the fins. A slow-moving species, it is easily intimidated by more active tankmates and may not always get its share of food.

MARBLED HATCHETFISH
Carnegiella strigata

Of a distinctly different shape, these hatchetfish grow to 1.5 inches. They occupy the upper area of the tank and can easily jump from uncovered aquariums. Like all hatchetfish, they should be kept in a group with quiet, placid tankmates. A water temperature of 74 to 82 degrees Fahrenheit with a pH of 5.5 to 7.5 and moderately soft to mildly hard water are recommended. Flake and freeze-dried foods are suitable. They will also appreciate tall plants with broad trailing leaves where they can find some shade.

ZEBRA DANIO
Brachydanio rerio

This small fish, reaching 1.5 inches when fully grown, is a schooling species that swims rapidly about the tank. It is hardy and peaceful but may disturb quiet species with its lively activity. A water temperature in the range of 68 to 78 degrees Fahrenheit, a pH of 6.5 to 8.0, and water that is soft to moderately hard are acceptable. This fish takes all flake and freeze-dried foods.

The Zebra Danio originates from India. With its bright blue bands separated by flashy strips of gold or silver and its almost constant activity, it will enhance any community tank.

WHITE CLOUD MOUNTAIN MINNOW
Tanichthys albonubes

A perfect beginner's fish, this species grows to a length of 1.5 inches and is peaceful and undemanding. It should be kept in a group and looks best in a tank with dark gravel and background. This species prefers somewhat cooler temperatures—65 to 75 degrees Fahrenheit—and a pH of 6.0 to 8.0 with soft to relatively hard water. It will do well on flake and freeze-dried foods.

This species comes from China, where it inhabits mountain streams. The Meteor Minnow, a very attractive long-finned variety of this hardy species, is sometimes available. Females are just a bit fuller or plumper than the males.

HARLEQUIN RASBORA
Rasbora heteromorpha

This quiet species grows to 1.5 inches and is best kept in small groups. Dark aquascaping and subdued light suit it best. As long as the water temperature is between 74 and 82 degrees Fahrenheit, the pH between 6.0 and 7.0, and the water moderately soft, this fish will do well. Flake and freeze-dried foods will provide a sufficient diet.

This fish is a muddled orange and pink with a prominent blue-black wedge that starts midbody and tapers back to the tail. The coloring is usually more pronounced in the males. A small, timid fish, it should not be kept with more active or aggressive species.

SCISSORTAIL RASBORA
Rasbora trilineata

Scissortails are a larger species that will reach three inches and do well when kept in a school of six or eight. They should have adequate swimming space and darkish aquascaping. They are a hardy fish and will do well at a water temperature between 72 and 82 degrees Fahrenheit with a pH between 6.0 and 6.5 and moderately soft water. All flake and freeze-dried foods are accepted.

The coloring of this species is rather bland, but they're worth keeping for their behavior and size. As large, active swimmers, they are an obvious presence in the tank. They are also skillful jumpers, so keep a tight-fitting lid on their tank. Their habit of repeatedly flicking their sharply forked tail fins adds interest and accounts for their common name.

ROSY BARB
Barbus conchonius

Like most barbs, this hardy, peaceful species is an active swimmer. It grows to 2.5 inches and should have a spacious tank. This fish does best at a somewhat cooler water temperature, in the range of 68 to 74 degrees Fahrenheit. A pH of 6.5 to 8.0 and water that is moderately soft to relatively hard are suitable. It will take flake and freeze-dried foods and should receive additional vegetable flake food as well. Males have decidedly darker fins than the females, and when they're ready to breed the males take on a deep pink hue. A long-finned variety of the Rosy Barb is also available.

BLACK RUBY BARB
Barbus nigrofasciatus

This very hardy species grows to two inches and needs plenty of room to swim. It also likes to have plants at the back and sides of the tank to take shelter in. The water temperature should be in the range of 72 to 82 degrees Fahrenheit with a pH of 6.0 to 7.5 and moderately soft to mildly hard water. It does well on all flake and freeze-dried foods.

Adult males are darker than females, and at breeding time their red coloration is greatly enhanced. Sometimes when males are kept together in a group, they will keep their breeding colors, perhaps as a form of competition.

TIGER BARB
Barbus tetrazona

An active, schooling species, this fish grows to two inches and needs a spacious tank for swimming. It has a reputation as a fin-nipper and should not be kept with slow-moving fish with long finnage such as gouramis. It is less likely to harass other fish when it is kept in a group; it may feel more secure that way, or it may simply be focusing its attention on the other members of the school. The Tiger Barb does well in a water temperature of 72 to 82 degrees Fahrenheit and a pH of 6.5 to 7.8 with moderately soft to relatively hard water. This fish will take all flake and freeze-dried foods.

CHERRY BARB
Barbus titteya

This beautiful species originates from Sri Lanka. It is not as active as other barbs, often hiding among the plants. The tank should be aquascaped with dark gravel, and the lighting should be subdued. Floating plants can be used to reduce the brightness. This fish tends to stay in the lower portion of the tank, whereas most other barbs prefer the middle and upper regions of the tank. A water temperature between 72 and 82 degrees Fahrenheit with a pH of 6.5 to 7.5 and moderately soft to somewhat hard water work well. Feed flake and freeze-dried foods.

GOLDEN BARB
Barbus 'schuberti'

The Golden Barb grows to 2.5 inches and should be kept in a shoal. This fish needs a large open area for swimming surrounded by plants. A water temperature between 72 and 82 degrees Fahrenheit, a pH of 6.5 to 8.0, and soft to moderately hard water are acceptable. It will do well on flake and freeze-dried foods.

This particular barb is unique in that its origin is unknown. It may actually be a color variation of the Chinese Barb, *Barbus semifasciolatus,* and not a separate species at all, which is why the species name appears in quotation marks.

RED-TAILED SHARK
Epalzeorhynchus bicolor

This species is not really a shark, despite its triangular dorsal fin and its common name. It grows to a length of five inches and is not particularly fond of its own kind. Either just one or a group of at least four or five should be kept in a tank. It is best to provide hiding places, and the fish prefers to have strong currents in the tank. This is among the more attractive bottom dwellers, but its color will fade in poor-quality water. A water temperature of 74 to 82 degrees Fahrenheit, a neutral pH of 6.8 to 7.2, and water that is moderately soft to slightly hard are suitable. It does well on flake and freeze-dried foods.

CLOWN LOACH
Botia macrantha

This beautiful fish grows to at least five inches and does best in groups. Numerous hiding places must be available. Hobbyists can find this fish at smaller, less-expensive sizes during certain times of the year. An attractive bottom dweller, this fish has the unusual habit of swimming with other species that display similar markings, such as Tiger Barbs. This species does well in a temperature range of 74 to 82 degrees Fahrenheit, a pH of 6.0 to 7.5, and soft to moderately hard water. It takes flake and freeze-dried foods but will also devour any snails in the tank.

COOLIE LOACH
Acanthopthalmus kuhli

This bottom-dwelling fish grows to three inches and does best when kept in a group. It does not do very well with active tankmates that also tend to spend their time at the bottom of the tank. It hides during the day, burying itself in gravel or finding shelter among plants, and comes out after the lights are turned off. This fish has an interesting color pattern and an atypical elongated shape. A water temperature of 72 to 82 degrees Fahrenheit along with a pH of 6.0 to 7.0 and soft to moderately hard water are fine. It takes all flake and freeze-dried foods, but should be fed only after the lights are off so that the other fish don't consume the food before it gets any.

GLASS CATFISH
Kryptopterus bicirrhis

Although popular, this species, which grows to four inches, is not as hardy as many of the other fish listed here. It must be kept in a group in a spacious tank with subdued lighting. The water temperature should be in the range of 72 to 82 degrees Fahrenheit with a pH between 6.0 and 7.5 and moderately soft to mildly hard water. In addition to flake and freeze-dried foods, live brine shrimp should be offered on a regular basis.

Remarkably, this species is almost transparent. Its internal organs are crowded together at the front of the body and are clearly visible. A midwater swimmer, it is most comfortable hiding in vegetation, so an abundance of plants may reduce stress.

PICTUS CAT
Pimelodella pictus

An active species that grows to six inches in length, this catfish should be kept in a tank with subdued lighting and several hiding places in the aquascaping. It can be kept alone but makes a nice display in a small group. A water temperature between 72 and 76 degrees Fahrenheit along with a pH in the range of 5.8 to 7.5 and moderately soft to somewhat hard water are best. It will eat pellet, tablet, flake, and freeze-dried foods, but it should be fed at night. This catfish will chase and eat most any fish that are small enough to swallow, so it's not suitable for all community aquariums.

UPSIDE-DOWN CATFISH
Synodontis nigriventris

As its common name implies, this species of catfish will swim upside down. One theory accounts for this unusual behavior as a feeding strategy. In the wild, it often grazes on the underside of submerged branches and logs, and swimming upside down makes these areas more accessible. Although it can be kept alone, it does much better when several are together. Like most catfish, it tends to hide during the day and become active at night, so adequate hiding spaces must be provided. It grows to 3.5 inches and does well at a water temperature in the range of 72 to 82 degrees Fahrenheit with a pH of 6.5 to 7.5 and water that is moderately soft to mildly hard. All flake and freeze-dried foods are eaten; they should be offered at night.

STRIPED RAPHAEL CATFISH
Platydoras costatus

This species will grow to eight inches and should be kept in a tank with larger community fish. They are active at night, hiding during the day. When the tank light is turned off and a night light in the room is on, these active fish can be observed along with any other catfish in the tank. This species does best at a water temperature between 74 and 86 degrees Fahrenheit and a pH in the range of 5.8 to 7.5 with moderately soft to somewhat hard water. All flake and freeze-dried foods are taken, although larger specimens will benefit from pellet foods.

BRONZE CATFISH
Corydoras aeneus

Over a dozen species of *Corydoras* are usually available in stores, but the Bronze Catfish is an excellent representative of that whole group. This small fish, growing to a length of 2.5 inches, is peaceful and active both at night and during the day. It is very social, and at least two or three should be kept together. A water temperature between 72 and 82 degrees Fahrenheit, a pH of 6.0 to 8.0, and water ranging from moderately soft to relatively hard are suitable. It eats all flake and freeze-dried foods and is particularly fond of live or frozen blackworms. Although it will consume any excess food in a tank, make sure this fish receives adequate amounts to eat.

STRIPE-TAILED CATFISH
Dianema urostriata

This peaceful, schooling fish grows to 4.5 inches. Subdued tank lighting and numerous hiding places in the tank are needed for this species, which becomes active at night. The water temperature should be between 72 and 80 degrees Fahrenheit with a pH in the range of 5.5 to 7.0 and moderately soft water. This fish will consume all flake and freeze-dried foods, but it should receive live brine shrimp as well.

A hefty little catfish, this species comes from South America's Amazon River. It has not yet bred in captivity, so aquarists must depend on wild-caught specimens for their tanks.

SPOTTED PLECO
Hypostomus punctatus

This is just one of many suckermouth catfish that will remove algae from flat surfaces in the tank. Some hobbyists find this species to be a nuisance, though, because of the way they rearrange aquascaping. Their bulk and careless swimming habits can uproot plants and overturn stones.

The Pleco grows to 12 inches and requires hiding places. A water temperature between 68 and 78 degrees Fahrenheit, a pH from 5.8 to 7.5, and soft to moderately hard water are fine. These fish should have substantial amounts of vegetable material in their diet. In addition to pellet and tablet foods, sliced zucchini boiled just long enough for it to sink should also be offered.

BRISTLENOSE CATFISH
Ancistrus temmincki

Another suckermouth catfish, this species reaches a length of 5.5 inches. It is hardy as long as good water quality and adequate amounts of vegetable material are provided. The water temperature should be between 70 and 80 degrees Fahrenheit with a pH of 6.5 to 7.5 and moderately soft to mildly hard water. All commercial foods are accepted, but parboiled, sliced zucchini and cooked peas should also be offered.

Males and females are easily distinguished. The males have an elaborate array of branched and forked tentacles on the head and around the upper jaw. The females have tentacles, too, but they are arranged in a neat row around the mouth and are not nearly as prominent.

DWARF SUCKING CATFISH
Otocinclus affinis

This is a small suckermouth catfish, growing to 1.5 inches. It is active during the day if there are hiding places among the plants. A water temperature between 68 and 78 degrees Fahrenheit, a pH between 5.5 and 7.2, and water that is relatively soft to moderately hard will be fine. Although it does consume algae on the plant leaves and tank glass, this fish also needs to have flake foods with a high vegetable matter content.

Some hobbyists feel that this is the ideal algae-eater for community aquariums. This species does the job well without disturbing plants, it's small and inconspicuous, and it doesn't disturb its tankmates.

DWARF RAINBOWFISH
Melanotaenia maccullochi

This hardy species grows to three inches in length. It is a schooling fish that needs adequate swimming room and good water quality to do well. A water temperature in the range of 64 to 78 degrees Fahrenheit is fine along with a pH between 7.0 and 8.2 and moderately soft to rather hard water. All flake and freeze-dried foods are eaten.

The Dwarf Rainbowfish comes from northern Australia and Papua New Guinea. The yellow-green color on its flank is broken by seven brown dotted horizontal lines, and there is an unmistakable red splotch on the gills. Courting males temporarily display an intense bright yellow stripe on the forehead.

RED RAINBOWFISH

Glossolepis incisus

This deep-bodied species reaches a length of six inches and does best in groups. It requires a large tank with both swimming space and planted areas. This fish should be kept at a water temperature of 72 to 76 degrees Fahrenheit, with a pH between 7.0 and 7.5 and moderately hard water. Although it will accept flake and freeze-dried foods, live foods such as brine shrimp or blackworms should also be provided.

This species hails from Papua New Guinea. Females are a soft, pale golden color, while the males are a fiery red. As with the Dwarf Rainbowfish, males show a bright yellow blaze on the forehead during courting.

MADAGASCAN RAINBOWFISH

Bedotia geayi

This active, hardy shoaling fish grows to 3.5 inches and should be kept in a tank with ample swimming space. This species spends almost all of its time near the surface; it's a good choice for filling the upper levels of the aquarium. It likes to jump too, though, so a secure lid is necessary. A water temperature in the range of 72 to 78 degrees Fahrenheit, a pH between 7.0 and 8.0, and moderately soft to relatively hard water provide the best environment. All flake and freeze-dried foods can be used, but live brine shrimp should also be in its regular diet.

GUPPY

Poecilia reticulata

One of the most popular aquarium fish, the guppy is a live-bearer, meaning it does not lay eggs but produces live offspring. Although the wild form is occasionally seen in stores, most are selectively bred forms chosen for their color pattern or finnage. Males of the bred species can reach 1.5 inches, and females typically grow to about 2.5 inches. Unlike the hardy wild specimens, aquarium strains are sensitive to water quality. Aquarium conditions should include a water temperature between 72 and 82 degrees Fahrenheit with a pH of 7.0 to 8.5 and water that is moderately to relatively hard. All flake and freeze-dried foods are eaten, but live brine shrimp should also be offered regularly.

BLACK MOLLY
Poecilia hybrid

This species is a hybrid, a cross between the Sailfin Molly and the Short-finned Molly. It's probably the hardiest of all the mollies, but good water quality is still essential. It does best when a teaspoon of salt is added for each gallon of water, but not all other fish can tolerate this much salt; check with your dealer before altering the salinity of a community tank. A water temperature of 72 to 82 degrees Fahrenheit, a pH from 7.2 to 8.2, and water that is moderately to relatively hard are fine. All flake and freeze-dried foods are accepted, but flake foods high in vegetable content are essential. Mollies and other live-bearers enjoy occasional feedings of blanched zucchini.

PLATY
Xiphophorus maculatus

A popular, hardy species, the Platy grows to two inches and is available in a wide variety of colors. As with all live-bearers, they will breed freely in a community tank, but the young are almost always eaten by tankmates. These fish do best at a water temperature between 70 and 78 degrees Fahrenheit and a pH of 7.0 to 8.2, in water that is moderately hard. All flake and freeze-dried foods are eaten, but flake foods high in vegetable content must also be provided. Small amounts of algae in the tank will also be eaten.

VARIATUS PLATY
Xiphophorus variatus

Another species of platy, this fish is found less commonly in stores because some varieties don't acquire full coloration until almost mature. It does well in slightly cooler water than the species listed above—66 to 74 degrees Fahrenheit—with a pH between 7.0 and 8.2. Moderately to relatively hard water is best. All flake and freeze-dried foods are taken. Be sure to offer flake food with high vegetable content.

SWORDTAIL
Xiphophorus helleri

This live-bearer grows to 3.5 inches and appears in a variety of color patterns. It is hardy as long as excellent water quality and frequent partial water changes are provided. It is an accomplished jumper, so a full aquarium hood with close-fitting openings for the filter and heater should be used. Males can become aggressive toward each other, so a tank should hold only one. This species does well at a water temperature between 70 and 78 degrees Fahrenheit with a pH of 7.0 to 8.3 and water that is moderately to relatively hard. It will eat all flake and freeze-dried foods and should be offered live brine shrimp occasionally.

PARADISE FISH
Macropodus opercularis

This species was the first tropical aquarium fish imported into Europe about 150 years ago. Like bettas and gouramis, it is able to take air directly at the surface of the water because of a respiratory organ known as a labyrinth. This fish grows to four inches and should not be kept with any small species. A water temperature of 68 to 78 degrees Fahrenheit, a pH of 6.0 to 8.0, and soft to hard water are the only requirements for this hardy fish. All flake and freeze-dried foods are consumed, but an occasional feeding of blackworms should also be offered.

SIAMESE FIGHTING FISH
Betta splendens

This species has been bred for its incredible variety of colors and long, flowing finnage. They are a colorful and attractive addition to any tank, but problems can arise in keeping them. Males are highly aggressive with each other and can't be kept in the same tank. They are also quite aggressive toward females most of the time. Although a single male can be kept in a small community aquarium, it will likely be harassed by any fin-nippers. A water temperature of 76 to 86 degrees Fahrenheit, a pH between 6.0 and 8.0, and soft to moderately hard water are needed. Flake and freeze-dried foods high in protein are taken, as well as very small, floating pellet foods and live brine shrimp on occasion.

DWARF GOURAMI
Colisa lalia

This peaceful species grows to two inches and is well-suited to a community tank inhabited by other small, calm fish. This beautiful Indian fish is available in several different color varieties. Its colors are most intense in a tank with bright lighting but dark aquascaping and lots of plants. A water temperature of 72 to 82 degrees Fahrenheit with a pH of 6.0 to 7.5 and moderately soft to somewhat hard water are good. It eats all flake and freeze-dried foods. Vegetable flake foods and occasional feedings of live brine shrimp should be included in its diet.

PEARL GOURAMI
Trichogaster leeri

This beautiful, peaceful fish grows to four inches. Its deep body is heavily peppered with shimmering silver spots that extend into the fins. The tank should be spacious, with lots of plants and subdued lighting; floating plants can help to provide areas where the light is diffused. This fish does best when kept in pairs—a male and a female. It should not be kept with aggressive tankmates. The water temperature should be between 72 and 82 degrees Fahrenheit and the pH between 6.5 and 8.5. The water can range from relatively soft to quite hard. A variety of flake foods with high vegetable content and freeze-dried foods should be offered.

THREE-SPOT GOURAMI
Trichogaster trichopterus

Also known as the Blue Gourami, this fish can reach four inches and is very peaceful. There is a great deal of color and pattern variation within this species; some have even lost the spots that prompted its common name. It is perfect for beginners and does well in community tanks even when small fish are present. A water temperature between 72 and 82 degrees Fahrenheit, a pH in the range of 6.0 to 8.5, and soft to relatively hard water are fine for this species. It consumes all flake and freeze-dried foods.

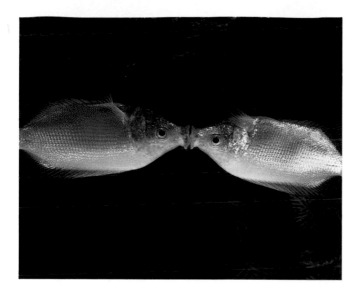

KISSING GOURAMI
Helostoma temmincki

Although this species can grow to 12 inches, in most tanks it only reaches about half that at the most. The "kissing" done by these fish is not a sign of affection; the behavior is used to settle minor disputes. Tank conditions should include a water temperature of 72 to 82 degrees Fahrenheit, a pH between 6.8 and 8.5, and soft to moderately hard water. All flake and freeze-dried foods are eaten, but a substantial amount of its diet should include vegetable flakes or, especially for larger fish, vegetable pellets and blanched zucchini.

ORANGE CHROMIDE
Etroplus maculatus

A member of the large, popular cichlid family, this fish grows to about three inches and fits comfortably in most community tanks. Although a hardy species overall, very small individuals are sometimes susceptible to fungus in pure fresh water. Adding a teaspoon of salt for each gallon of water eliminates the problem, but some hobbyists believe that certain tankmates, such as catfish and angelfish, do better without salt. A water temperature of 72 to 82 degrees Fahrenheit, a pH of 7.5 to 8.5, and hard to relatively hard water are best. All flake and freeze-dried foods are accepted, but they will nibble on live plants if they don't get fresh vegetable food regularly.

COMMON KRIB
Pelvicachromis pulcher

This peaceful African fish grows to 3.5 inches and is well-suited to a community tank as long as hiding places are provided. It is sensitive to problems with water quality and does best when the water is changed frequently. A water temperature in the range of 72 to 82 degrees Fahrenheit, a pH of 6.5 to 7.5, and moderately soft to mildly hard water are fine. All flake and freeze-dried foods are consumed. Females are smaller and chunkier than males, and they have shorter dorsal and anal fins.

SWALLOWTAIL CICHLID
Lamprologus brichardi

This very attractive cichlid that originated from Lake Tanganyika in East Africa is hardy enough for beginners. It grows to four inches and should be kept in a spacious tank with lots of rockwork and caves. Several striking color varieties are available. A water temperature from 72 to 82 degrees Fahrenheit, a pH between 7.5 and 8.5, and moderately hard to truly hard water will provide the best conditions. All flake and freeze-dried foods are accepted, but occasional feedings of live foods, such as brine shrimp, are highly recommended.

EGYPTIAN MOUTHBROODER
Pseudocrenilabrus multicolor

This small cichlid, which originates from the Nile River, will grow to 2.5 inches in length and is well suited for most community tanks. It is very peaceful as long as its companions are too large for it to swallow. The water temperature should be in the range of 68 to 78 degrees Fahrenheit with a pH between 6.8 and 8.2. Moderately soft to relatively hard water is acceptable. All flake and freeze-dried foods are eaten.

KEYHOLE CICHLID
Aequidens maronii

These very gentle, almost timid, cichlids grow to four inches and should be kept only with other peaceful fish. They have an irregular blotch on the side that resembles a keyhole, and they sometimes change color when startled. The tank should contain plants and driftwood to provide security and hiding places for the fish. A water temperature of 72 to 78 degrees Fahrenheit, a pH in the range of 6.5 to 7.5, and slightly soft to moderately hard water are best. They will eat all flake and freeze-dried foods and should have an occasional feeding of live brine shrimp.

RED-HUMPED EARTHEATER
Geophagus steindachneri

This South American cichlid can grow to six inches in a sufficiently large tank. It has a fierce appearance but is actually a rather peaceful species that can be kept in a community tank with other moderate-size fish. In the wild, it will root through muddy river bottoms looking for food. In the aquarium, it will root through the gravel, making it difficult to maintain live plants and impractical to use an undergravel unit for biological filtration. The water temperature should be in the range of 72 to 82 degrees Fahrenheit with a pH 6.5 to 7.2 and moderately soft to mildly hard water. All flake and freeze-dried foods are consumed, but as the fish increases in size, pellet and tablet foods should be offered as well.

ANGELFISH
Pterophyllum scalare

This very popular cichlid from the Amazon basin reaches a length of five inches and a height of eight inches. The distinctive shape of the body and fins adds variety to the community aquarium. The tank should be deep enough for the fish to swim comfortably with its fins extended. Although peaceful by cichlid standards, it will consume very small fish if given the opportunity. The water temperature should be between 74 and 82 degrees, with a pH between 5.8 and 7.5. Soft water is ideal, but even moderately hard water is acceptable. All flake and freeze-dried foods are eaten, but live or frozen foods should also be offered.

FIREMOUTH CICHLID
Cichlasoma meeki

This relatively peaceful species grows to five inches. It should not be kept with very small fish but otherwise is suitable for most community tanks. It can be somewhat territorial but poses no real threat to any good-sized tankmates. The fish has a brilliant red underside, a smoky gray upper body, and dark splotches scattered along its flanks. Water conditions should include a temperature in the range of 72 to 82 degrees Fahrenheit, a pH between 6.8 and 8.0, and moderately soft to slightly hard water. It can be fed all flake and freeze-dried foods, and will take pellets when it grows larger.

INDEX